The Purpose of Freedom
Published by Casting Seeds Publishing

Published in the United States by Casting Seeds Publishing an extension and aid to UNPLUGGED.

***

Websites and Social Media sites:
Website: IAMUNPLUGGED.COM | MYCOACHJOSH.COM
Social Media: **@MYCOACHJOSH**

COACH JOSH

TABLE OF CONTENTS

The purpose of freedom Intro - A warning from Coach Josh

This book is a book that I believe is going to be so beneficial and impactful in your life that I must initiate a warning. The contents of this book are going to give you formulas, perspectives, and scriptures to help you become free in whatever you are facing. I must warn you because of the contents of this book your enemy, the demons that have been assigned to you, are not going to want you to finish this book. I want you to set an atmosphere, I want you to carve out a time, I want you to establish a place so that you and God can engage with the materials in this book to help you walk in the freedom that Christ has given you. I challenge you today to be focused, to be diligent, and to really take your time through this book so that you will be able to understand what it's going to take for you to be free indeed.

Name: _____ Date Received: _____

CHAPTER ONE – THE FORMULA TO FREEDOM

Let's talk about the formula of freedom. There are a few things that I want to share with you;

1. the place of freedom,
2. the perverted freedom,
3. the plan of freedom,
4. the path to freedom,
5. the price of freedom, and
6. the purpose of freedom.

Let us start with the place of freedom. Community with God was the whole purpose of our creation; his presence is where joy and freedom lies. The number one thing that God desired for Him and his creation was for community and for us to enhance, build and protect that community. The whole purpose of our essence was for us to engage with our creator, so that our engagement with our creator will lead us to creating and inspiring others to create. That is why I tell people you have to know your purpose because the more you engage in your purpose the less likely you will fall into sin. In order to win, we must be too productive to sin. Productivity and creativity are only found, in its purest form, in the presence of God. The Bible says in Psalm 16 that in His presence there is a fullness of joy. Being absent from God's presence leads to depression, sadness, and pain. My question to you is are you happy or are you joyful? Happiness like you've heard me say many times is based upon conditions, that if this person is not in my life, if this thing is not in my life then I am not happy; or, if these things are, I am happy.

Joy says that it doesn't matter what I have or don't have, I am full of joy because I know in whom I believe. When you know God as a person and you are developing that community with him, then that place of freedom will be a go-to place for you to refuel, so that when life takes away your energy or when you give it you will always be refuelled by God. That's why the enemy wants you to be separated from God, through sin. When we are separated from God through sin that we practice knowingly, we miss out on opportunities to be refuelled, and we begin to sink in our pursuits of happiness instead of being content in the presence of God where there is a fullness of joy.

It's just like a cell phone service; just because you have a phone doesn't mean you have access. A payment gives you access. When a person fails to pay their phone bill it doesn't erase the service of the phone company it just erases their connection. When you are faithfully walking with God and trusting in His payment for your sins, you will always remain connected to His network. But when you begin to mismanage your relationship with him and try to pay for a connection with Him you will lose connection. The payment lies in what Jesus did 2,000 years ago. Since He paid I can now have a connection with the father but if I abuse that grace or do not embrace His payment I will be disconnected from its supply of creativity and nourishment.

Everywhere God is there is freedom, and there is joy. We become bound when we disconnect ourselves from that presence. Eden was that place. What Adam and Eve did in Eden is what we often do in our lives. Eden, in the beginning, was the place of freedom, there was no sin, there was no pain, there was no lust, there were no fears. Nothing sinful was there because God's presence was the climate, God's presence was the atmosphere. And the moment that Eve and Adam broke Covenant they were no longer fit for Eden's Holy Climate. See the thing that keeps us connected is the Covenant, and when we break Covenant we disconnect. When we begin to engage into certain things, unaware or aware, we begin to disconnect ourselves from the joy we need and the freedom that we need to progress.

Many believers fall short because they forget who they are connected to. Whoever you are connected to will determine the resources you have access to. That's why I am so thankful that God has allowed me to pursue access and not assets. Many people are after God's assets but careless about him as a person.

Eden was a place of freedom, but this freedom too had restrictions. People look at freedom as unlimited, but God's freedom is limited. God's grace is abundant, but even in its abundance there are specific limits. The reason why many of us do not understand freedom is because we don't know what it feels like to be free. It takes a certain level of understanding and appreciation to stay free. With this freedom, there are restrictions because God told Adam and Eve that you can eat from any tree in this garden, but this one. God is telling you right now you can enjoy everything in me, through me, and with me, but you can't enjoy certain things in this world. It is those thing that keeps us from enjoying the rest. It is sad that 1% of the garden is what we desire versus the abundance of enjoying the 99% of it. It is something about the human heart that desires to be like God whether consciously or subconsciously. Satan does not want God to be in his rightful place in your life; he wants you to try and control it or let him control it.

When you want to be in control of your life, you are telling God, "I want to be god over my life." You are incapable of making yourself free. It is only in the presence of God that you can be free, and you must fight for that place, you must maintain that place, you must be in love with that place. Where is that place where you and God can meet regularly? Do you have a place where you and God can meet every single day? Is there a place on your job? Can you be creative in discovering places whether in your car, at your workplace, before you go to the gym, where you can say I am just going to go here to refuel really quick? Yes, God is with us, he is Emmanuel, God with Us. But we've got to make sure we have real checkpoints in our lives that become little places where we can go just in case we get frustrated to refuel ourselves up. You notice hospitals and gas stations don't follow people or cars. You must have a place where you go to receive health and fuel. Those two places are designed for you to go to when you are aware that you are in need. Seek the place where God is!

What place could you and God meet regularly?	What are some checkpoint places you and God can meet to refuel outside of your regular meeting place?

Perverted Freedom

Let's talk about the perverted freedom. Satan offered Eve and offers every one of us a perverted freedom a freedom that leads to complete separation from God and enslavement to sin. Eve thought she was enslaved or bound by God, not knowing that the enemy was trying to tempt her into transferring her dominance and power into his hand. Satan at this moment in the text was not the most powerful; Adam and Eve were more powerful than him. He through suggestions came to Eve and Adam and made them transfer their dominance. God gave them dominion over everything on the Earth. And Satan understood that the best way for him to have dominion over the fish, dominion over the water, and dominion over the birds in the air, dominion over land, dominion over people is to get the very person who is holding the keys to that dominance to transfer it over.

He begins to suggest to her that possibly God is trying to keep her from being "completely" free. He was saying why is God restricting this tree from you? Why is he restricting you from the opportunity of knowing good and evil? Moreover, when she began to process that suggestion, she began to think that God was the slave master; she was beginning to think why would God keep such valuable information from me? And she thought that if I become equal with God that I will be completely free, that I can create my own world per se, that Adam and myself can create this new way of life disconnected from this slave master God, not knowing that she was taking herself and her husband away from a peaceful place of freedom. Yes, this freedom has restrictions, yes, this freedom says not to do this or that, and yes, this freedom says that you can have this, but you can't have that. But she thought, "I want it all."

Sometimes all should not be allocated to all. Because all takes a whole lot of management and if you are not God you are not going to be able to manage what only God can manage. And she thought I want to be equal with God and be able to manage what he manages. But what she failed to realize was that she was getting tricked into giving up her freedom for a perverted freedom; this happens all the time. Why is God saying I can't have sex before marriage? What do you mean I can't do this or that? Instead of trusting in God's original plan, I'm going to go and be free. As the prodigal son did – he said; "Pops I want you to give me my inheritance; I want you to give me what is owed to me". And what the prodigal son did to the father was let the father know 'I don't love you'. Because when someone asks for their inheritance, it's almost them asking the wishing of that person's death, seeing that you get an inheritance after someone dies. So this son was saying I wish you were dead, because once you are dead I can have my inheritance.

His demands were so insensitive seeing that his dad had to literally go and sell what was owed to his son. See back in the day they couldn't just go to a bank and get the money out and give the inheritance over, no, he had to go and sell whatever percentage of land that was due to his son, he had to go sell the land and the cattle. Not only did he wish that his father was dead, but he was also putting his father in debt. Because now he said I want you to sell everything that could make you profitable - land is profitable, animals are profitable, all these different things are profitable. And he went and took all of that and sold it and gave his son the inheritance. But you notice the father didn't follow the son when he left he allowed that son to leave trusting in God. The mindset of that son is similar to how many of us think we often times think that our lives will be better outside of our father's home than in our father's home. However, what we fail to realize, like this son, is that when we are outside of that safety net, outside of that presence and protection, there will always be danger. He also failed to realize that there would be people draining him of his inheritance, draining him of his creativity, putting him in a place far less than where he deserved, to the point that when he began to eat from the pig's pen he began to say that I had it better at my father's house than here.

The enemy wants you to leave God and go as far as you can and waste your inheritance. Do you know what you were inherently given? When Christ died we received an inheritance when Christ rose he validated that inheritance - he gave us life, a connection, a sense of purpose, grace, and even freedom. From that moment, many believers and many people have been mismanaging that inheritance; they have squandered their creativity, given their musical talents, their athletic talents, their intellectual talents over to the world. They have been allowing people to drain them dry. Instead of eating filet mignon in their father's house, they're eating rubbish from pig pens.

And God is saying when are you going to come back home? When are you going to realize that sin cannot sustain you? The beautiful thing about this story was when the son came back to the father the father wasn't upset. It is so sad that it's the other sons that hinder the weaker sons per se from being free. And that's what's keeping people from coming back to their father because God's other children is trying to guard that presence. But I am so thankful that our heavenly father loves us and welcomes us back to his place of freedom and enables us to forsake Satan's perverted freedom. When the prodigal son came back home they killed a fatted calf; they prepared a meal. And God says when you come back to his place of freedom you will be free indeed, and that everything that you have done has been forgotten. This perverted freedom that Eve and Adam partook of placed them into slavery. Anything or anyone outside of God leads to slavery; that's why his presence is important because in his presence there is salvation from slavery.

The Plan of Freedom

Let's talk about the plan of freedom. The plan was for God and man to be reconciled and to provide a system that will allow a holy God to engage with unholy individuals, individuals who were marred by sin. The plan was for God to take the penalty of man so that the cost of what happened in Eden which was expensive could be paid for. All of mankind could each work 1,000 years and still could not pay what we owe for destroying his creation. Imagine how you would feel if someone came into your house, in a house that took six days or six months or six years to make and in 60 seconds it was destroyed, separating you from your home for some time; you wouldn't appreciate it. That's what happened in creation. It took six days for God to create the world, and in a matter of 60 seconds to six minutes it was destroyed. The same feeling you would have felt if someone destroyed what you love the most, is the same feeling that God has about sin. But I am so thankful that God's perspective on sin is not just a wrathful one or an angered one, but it is one that desires to be reconnected. The plan of freedom was for us to be reconciled through Christ's work on the cross back to God and back into freedom.

But many of us have forsaken that plan for our own plans. What are you doing right now that is destroying what God created?

The plan of freedom was an amazing plan that he even warned about this when he had a conversation with Adam, Eve and the serpent before his plan went into motion. Some people will say why would God go through so much just for this? Why would he create Satan, and why would he have put a tree in the garden when we would have been okay without it all? But for love to be proven, love must be tested. And God said I had to put a tree amidst your life to prove if and to show how much you truly love me. True freedom is when you can look at something that once had you bound and confidently say no to it, not even wrestle with it and walk away. If you wrestle with it, you still have some love for it, but if you have the power to walk away, you love God more. This plan that God had for us was powerful.

The Path to Freedom

Let's talk about the path to freedom. The path to freedom will require a holy conception, a holy life, a holy death and a holy resurrection. It's crazy how God created the woman's womb to separate itself from the child. God even created the woman's womb before the woman even fell for his path. He created a path in a woman that would separate the baby from the woman, from blood transferring, so that when it was time for Jesus to step on the scene the Holy Spirit could place a holy seed inside of an unholy ground, because he knew that the seed would be supplied by a holy and sanctified source.

And that's why it required a holy and unblemished conception - meaning that the conception inside of Mary had to be so holy that when Jesus was lodged within this unholy womb that the blood of the woman could not get into the blood of the son so that the son could still be truly God and truly man. It also required a holy life; he had to live perfect. For him to have a perfect life there had to have been a perfect conception, and if there was a perfect conception there had to have been a perfect plan. He had to live a life tempted but not giving his power over to it. He had to live a life where the Bible says he was tempted and tested at every point so that we can have a high priest that understands. He knows what it feels like to be rejected, to be tempted, to be tested, to be offended and to be murdered.

The path to freedom included God wrapping himself in flesh and being amongst us. God had to wrap himself in what we are wrapped in so that he could be able to know what it is like to be us. A holy God with no flesh didn't know what it was like to be cold or hot; He didn't know what it was like to feel pain seeing that pain and negative feelings came through the fall. Jesus never fell therefore he doesn't know what it is like to be fallen. But because he fell from heaven into earth and wrapped himself in the flesh, he now could walk in this world and feel what it is like to be cold, to be hot, to feel alone, to feel rejected, to feel pain, to feel abused, to feel death. He lived amongst us so that he would know what it is like to be us.

I'll give an example - Jesus was like NBA 2K before NBA 2K, meaning that he created himself as a created player in another dimension and was completely dependent on God the Father who held the controller and played a perfect game. That yes Jesus the son and God the heavenly father are one, it's as if you were playing a created player, except for when we mess up with a steal, or we throw the ball out of bounds, or we miss a rebound, etc. that game is not perfect. But because Jesus only did what he saw his father do he was able, controlled by God to live a perfect life.

The Price of Freedom

Let's talk about the price of freedom. The price of freedom was gruesome. It required the complete mutilation and humiliation of Jesus. Not only should we understand the place of freedom being Eden, the perverted freedom that came in the form of a suggestion, the plan of freedom that was in the heart of God and the path to freedom through Jesus, but we must also know the significance of the price. The price of freedom will let us know how we should through love stay in the place of freedom. The reason why many people are not appreciative of that place is because they weren't there to see what it cost. He gave his time, he gave wisdom, and he gave three powerful years of his life. He was betrayed, he was falsely accused, and was beaten so severely that he was unrecognizable, he was crucified and buried but rose. He paid the payment we owed and we ranged up the tab, meaning that the price was so high that his death paid the price of everyone who sinned before him, everyone who was sinning during his life on earth, and those who sinned beyond him. That tab was so high, but he paid it anyway.

Why does this price matter? It matters because all of us are responsible for the murder of Jesus seeing that his death had to pay for the sins of everyone. Each one of us is guilty of murder. That's why the gospel matters, that's why we must fight hard to stay in that place. When we don't know the place of this freedom, the perverted freedom that is after our attention, the plan of freedom, the path to freedom, the price of that freedom, we will not know the purpose of this freedom.

The Purpose of Freedom

What were we freed from and what are we freed for?

We were freed from sin and freed for sanctification, meaning that through what Christ did for us we are now freed from sin and that we actually have the capability and the capacity through the spirit of God to be able to avoid sin. That's why I tell people you have the power to overcome sin in a matter of seconds. But your awareness of that power determines how long you execute. If I know I am freed from sin, and I am tempted to sin, I know for a fact that I have the power through the spirit of God, not in my own power, to be able to overcome it, that's why sanctification is important. We are freed from sin, but we are freed for

18

sanctification, meaning that sanctification is purifying us, maturing us, putting us in position to be able to be strengthened. Without sanctification there is no strength, without no pruning, there is no strength. And we need that sanctification to be able to become knowledgeable and strengthened through the precious spirit of God and becoming more aware of how we can always overcome and trump sin.

But the sad thing is many people are still sitting in that open cage and not walking in freedom. Is that you? Are you still sitting bound by pornography, bound by sexual desires, bound by insecurity, bound in un-forgiveness, bound in bitterness? Are you still sitting in that cage and allowing the suggestions of your neighbours to keep you in the cage when God has set you free? For freedom Christ has set us free. Stand for him therefore and do not submit again to a yoke of slavery. God desires for us to be free, to stand firm and not submit again to the yoke of slavery. We have to understand that sin equals slavery. We are all slaves; at least be a slave to a gentle master.

In order for us to appreciate the love of God, we must first understand the wrath of God. The number one thing that God desires to save the whole world from is not our sins or the sins of others or even hell. The number one thing he desires to save us from is from himself. Many people focus so much on John 3:16 but avoid the contents of the entire chapter. Let us dig in!

John 3 You Must Be Born Again

3 Now there was a man of the Pharisees named Nicodemus, a ruler of the Jews. 2 This man came to Jesus by night and said to him, "Rabbi, we know that you are a teacher come from God, for no one can do these signs that you do unless God is with him." 3 Jesus answered him, **"Truly, truly, I say to you, unless one is born again he cannot see the kingdom of God."** *4 Nicodemus said to him, "How can a man be born when he is old? Can he enter a second time into his mother's womb and be born?" 5 Jesus answered,* **"Truly, truly, I say to you, unless one is born of water and the Spirit, he cannot enter the kingdom of God. 6 That which is born of the flesh is flesh, and that which is born of the Spirit is spirit.** *7 Do not marvel that I said to you, 'You must be born again.' 8 The wind blows where it wishes, and you hear its sound, but you do not know where it comes from or where it goes. So it is with everyone who is born of the Spirit." 9 Nicodemus said to him, "How can these things be?" 10 Jesus answered him, "Are you the teacher of Israel and yet you do not understand these things? 11 Truly, truly, I say to you, we speak of what we know, and bear witness to what we have seen, but you do not*

receive our testimony. 12 If I have told you earthly things and you do not believe, how can you believe if I tell you heavenly things? 13 No one has ascended into heaven except he who descended from heaven, the Son of Man 14 And as Moses lifted up the serpent in the wilderness, so must the Son of Man be lifted up, 15 that whoever believes in him may have eternal life.

16 **"For God so loved the world, that he gave his only Son, that whoever believes in him should not perish but have eternal life. 17 For God did not send his Son into the world to condemn the world, but in order that the world might be saved through him**. 18 Whoever believes in him is not condemned, but whoever does not believe is condemned already, because he has not believed in the name of the only Son of God. **19 And this is the judgment: the light has come into the world, and people loved the darkness rather than the light because their works were evil. 20 For everyone who does wicked things hates the light and does not come to the light, lest his works should be exposed. 21 But whoever does what is true comes to the light, so that it may be clearly seen that his works have been carried out in God."**

22 After this Jesus and his disciples went into the Judean countryside, and he remained there with them and was baptizing. 23 John also was baptizing at Aenon near Salim, because water was plentiful there, and people were coming and being baptized 24 (for John had not yet been put in prison).

25 Now a discussion arose between some of John's disciples and a Jew over purification. 26 And they came to John and said to him, "Rabbi, he who was with you across the Jordan, to whom you bore witness—look, he is baptizing, and all are going to him." 27 John answered, "A person cannot receive even one thing unless it is given him from heaven. 28 You yourselves bear me witness, that I said, 'I am not the Christ, but I have been sent before him.' 29 The one who has the bride is the bridegroom. The friend of the bridegroom, who stands and hears him, rejoices greatly at the bridegroom's voice. Therefore, this joy of mine is now complete. 30 He must increase, but I must decrease."

31 He who comes from above is above all. He who is of the earth belongs to the earth and speaks in an earthly way. He who comes from heaven is above all. 32 He bears witness to what he has seen and heard, yet no one receives his testimony. 33 Whoever receives his testimony sets his seal to this, that God is true. 34 For he whom God has sent utters the words of God, for he gives the Spirit without measure. **35 The Father loves the Son and has given all things into his**

hand. 36 Whoever believes in the Son has eternal life; whoever does not obey the Son shall not see life, but the wrath of God remains on him.

Let's break down the importance of the scriptures that are barely mentioned out of John 3.

- *"Truly, truly, I say to you, unless one is born again he cannot see the kingdom of God."*
- *"Truly, truly, I say to you, unless one is born of water and the Spirit, he cannot enter the kingdom of God. 6 That which is born of the flesh is flesh, and that which is born of the Spirit is spirit.*

The Chapter begins with a conversation between Jesus and a Pharisee named Nicodemus over the topic of salvation. The two scriptures above highlights key points that Jesus made to Nicodemus and makes to us all. His first statement was that in order for us to see the salvation of God and to enter the kingdom of God we must be born again. Many people gloss over what it really means to be born again. In order for you and me to enter, the kingdom of God there must be a real conversion. There must be a new birth in our hearts. Without this tangible miracle no can reap the benefits of the kingdom of God. He continues to say that unless we are born of water and the Spirit we cannot enter the kingdom of God. The water represents baptism and the imputed righteousness of Jesus and the Spirit represents the sealing of the authentic work of the spirit of God. Let us continue.

- *16 "For God so loved the world, that he gave his only Son, that whoever believes in him should not perish but have eternal life.*
- *17 For God did not send his Son into the world to condemn the world, but in order that the world might be saved through him.*

The famous verse John 3:16 has been heralded as the verse of all versus highlighting the salvation of humanity but it also has been sliced away from other versus that highlights real reasons on why billions of people have yet to be impacted by this verse. Verse 16 highlights God's love and Gods plan; it says that God so loved the world (not the worlds system but the people of the world) that he gave his only son (meaning his only perfect option) so that whosoever would believe in him would not perish but will have everlasting life. The word "believe" in modern day Christianity has been overused and devalued. People make it sound like it is that easy to be saved. Anybody can confess Jesus as Lord but how many people have really made Him their lord? The hyperemotional experiences of modern day Christianity has devalued the word "believe", and all you hear is just believe in Jesus but what about the auditing of a genuine conversion, what about seeking for fruit behind the leaves, what about helping people process what it means to deny oneself and take up their cross to follow Jesus all the way through? Like vs. eight of John 3 says,

8 The wind blows where it wishes, and you hear its sound, but you do not know where it comes from or where it goes. So it is with everyone who is born of the Spirit."

Meaning that salvation is one, God's doing and two, specifically random. The wind you can hear but you cannot see and its direction is unaware. Nevertheless, in order for there to be belief there must be a beckoning or a drawing by the Spirit of God that drifts us into uttering the phrase "I Believe that Jesus is the son of God I repent of all my sins and I desire to welcome him into my life as my saviour and my Lord." However, when you sell experiences instead of offering the Gospel you will get a lot of utterances but not a lot of conversions. God uses a series of life situations to beckon his chosen people into a real belief that will be measured by the fruit of the spirit that stems from them walking in the spirit. Nothing in life is free and that includes your salvation. Your salvation requires you to give up your life. It may not cost you a dime but it does cost you your life and not too many people are willing to pay that price. So many people advertise the Love of God but never explain to you the stipulations of it which are in the versus below

- *19 And this is the judgment: the light has come into the world, and people loved the darkness rather than the light because their works were evil. 20 For everyone who does wicked things hates the light and does not come to the light, lest his works should be exposed. 21 But whoever does what is true comes to the light, so that it may be clearly seen that his works have been carried out in God."*

Jesus is the light of the world and only those who desire to be changed will be drawn to it because they will want to know what is in them that could be used against God working in and through them. But those who deep down do not love God will do whatever it takes to avoid the light of the real Jesus and will create a false Jesus to sit up under. The verse reads that these individuals love darkness more than the light because their works were evil. Meaning that many people truly do not want Jesus and if you look at their lives closely there is no proof anywhere of a conversion. The fruit of conversion is the desire to be close to God and in order for us to be close to God we have to be in his light and if we are in his light then we will always see reasons to improve and our improvements will prove a genuine connection with God. No improvement no proof of salvation. It even says that those who practice wicked things hate the light meaning they hate Jesus. Many fake believers may not say it out of their mouth but they do so through their lives. Those who love God do not mind being exposed but those who mind being exposed do not genuinely love God. The proof is in what you are unwilling to let Go. What sins are you practicing wilfully without remorse?

- 35 The Father loves the Son and has given all things into his hand. 36 Whoever believes in the Son has eternal life; whoever does not obey the Son shall not see life, but the wrath of God remains on him.

Finally verse 35 this verse talks about the results of belief and non-belief. For those who have been beckoned into belief and who are bearing fruit with keeping with repentance will have eternal life but those who do not obey the son shall not see life and the wrath of God remains on him. If that does not send chills down your spine, I do not know what else will. Those who do not obey God out of love have not been converted by his love and if his love has not converted them then his WRATH REMAINS ON THEM! When you understand that God hates sin and abhors those who through pride practice it then you will do whatever it takes to check your heart. His wrath remains on those who practice unrighteousness and when you know that God is the ultimate judge and that he sees all and knows all then you who truly understand honour will respect him. He is not a person to be scared of just a person to be respected. Yes, he loves you but with all loving relationships there is a choice and if you choose to stay married to the world then you will suffer the punishment of the world and that's eternity in Hell and eternally separated from God. It is like a relationship that has gone bad due to infidelity. The one who cheated or wants out of a good relationship feels great in the beginning because he or she wants freedom. They want to be separated forever from their spouse and live freely. While they are living freely, they begin to recognize the quality of life they now have without the one they use to be in relationship with. They begin to recognize how uneven their life is and desires to want them back. They call multiple times to get an answer and when their ex-wife or husband finally picks up they begin to beg them to get back with them. However, while that person was away living their best/worst life their ex got with someone that cherished them and responded on the phone that they were getting married again. They both get off the phone and the one that cheated or wanted out has to now live-forever separated from the love of their life. The same is with some of us that will find out too late, about who God desired to be with us. I say some because many people will hit hell wide open with so much pride that they would rather suffer in hell then to live with God. But there will be some that will have to reminisce on the countless opportunities they had to truly believe. What is hovering over you God's grace or God's wrath? Check your heart.

***

Scriptures on Freedom.

2 Corinthians 3:17 - *Now the Lord is the spirit, and where the spirit of the Lord is there is freedom.* God is a spirit and the core of us is spirit. When we allow our spirits to connect to his we experience true freedom. That's why it is important for us to submit our spirits to the leading of the Holy Spirit so that we can continue to walk in Freedom. We must never forget that God's spirit will never fully operate through a person who is habitually practicing sin. His spirit is there to convict us before sinning and to comfort us after repenting for it but it does not engage with a person that is completely committed to sinning. You can't be committed to God and committed to your sins. You have to make a choice. Will you make mistakes sure but I heard from somewhere that when we make a mistake the first time, it is a mistake but if we do it again it is a choice. What are you choosing to do?

Another thing that helps with being free and walking out of that cage is **John 8:31-38** - *So Jesus said to the Jews who had believed him, 'If you abide in my word you are truly my disciples and you will know the truth and the truth will set you free'. They answered him, 'We are offspring's of Abraham and we have never been enslaved to anyone. How is it that you say you will become free?' Jesus answered them, 'Truly truly I say to you everyone who practices sin is a slave to sin. The slave does not remain in the house forever, the son remains forever, so if the son sets you free you will be free indeed. I know that you are offspring's of Abraham yet you seek to kill me because my word finds no place in you. I speak of what I have seen with my father and you do what you have heard from your father.*

Here are some points - the word of God leads to freedom. You have to take him at his word. If he is true, then his words are true. Adhering to his word leads to discipline which proves we are his disciple, and the longer we remain in him the more we will know the truth. And everyone who allows the truth to take reign, that truth will set them free in that area. What area in your life have you yet allowed truth to enter? When you allow truth to enter you will be set free. That truth is a capital T because that truth is a person. When you accept him as the truth, the answer to everything will follow and you will truly be free, not only free indeed as far as really being free, but free in your deeds meaning in your actions. Meaning you will be free to do things the right way and freed from doing things wrongly. Many people are bound because they either don't know the truth or they know the truth but ignore it. Do you know the truth, or are you ignoring him? Don't boast of any sort of freedom outside of Jesus.

Verse 33 - they began to talk as if Abraham was the one who set them free. Abraham, your mom, your dad, and your accomplishments are not your source of freedom. Anything outside of Jesus can lead to bondage. Jesus answers their request by saying whoever practices sin will remain a slave to that sin. He also said that the truth will always remain, not those that are enslaved to sin, meaning that he will last forever. And he begins to say if the son sets you free you are free indeed, meaning if you allow him to set you free you will be free forever.

This book is designed to help you understand the process of freedom. Today if you have accepted Christ you are free. But freedom is also your responsibility. God created Eden, a place for his people to be free. Once the people acted against God, their freedom was even more restricted. But because of what Christ did on the cross we now have access to that place again, that presence again. We no longer have to hear stories that the Holy Spirit came upon this person or that person, but now the Holy Spirit is within us all who are saved, that his presence is not just external, but his presence is internal, and we now have access to this freedom. Are you ready to be freed today? If so turn the page.

CHAPTER TWO – WHAT ARE SOUL TIES AND STRONGHOLDS

Each one of us have either experienced or are experiencing the effects of a soul tie or a stronghold. But before I go deeper into these themes let's consider some definitions.

Soul-tie:
A soul-tie is any internal connection a person has to a person, place, product or perspective whether properly or improperly.

Stronghold:
A stronghold is the final stage of a perverted soul-tie leading to mental barriers that a person cannot pass.

Let's now give these two themes images. Soul ties and strongholds are designed to be ropes, roots, and restrictions. They are designed to tie us, anchor us and restrict us. Satan's goal is to keep us from progressing in the things of God. He wants us tied to a past memory, rooted in emotions and restricted by fears. He understands that if I can utilize something as small as a thought to tie you inwardly, then I don't have to use much to tie you outwardly. It's crazy how many of us are tied by something as small as a thought. Thoughts are heavier than we think. They bombard our minds hoping to gain ground with the intent to bear demonic fruit. See every thought is a seed and if planted will produce a harvest. What kind of seeds are in your mind?

The Bible talks early in Genesis 6 about seeds it says that as the earth remains there will be seed, time and harvest. This formula is throughout life. Let's take some time and discuss this Biblical formula in the context of our individual lives.

This formula seed, time and harvest was designed to ensure growth and to ensure everything in the seed continues to thrive forever. Without this formula active and protected everything that was designed to be good for humanity dies. Every seed has within it; potential. It has the potential to be a tree, a forest, and food. Based on where it is planted will determine if it will meet its potential. Just because it has potential doesn't mean it will produce. It all boils down to where it's planted. It's amazing how something as small as a seed has so much in it. The same goes with our thoughts. In order for a regular seed and a thought to grow their needs to be a set time. Without this set time the seed will produce either no return or a premature return. In order for there to be a harvest, there must be a set time to govern its predestined process. God desires for our minds and hearts to only receive good seed. He desires for us to only think on what is true, what is honourable, what is just, what is pure, what is lovely, what is commendable (Phil 4:8) so that these traits will be manifested in our lives. Satan has a counter formula design to suffocate this good mental formula. His formula is suggestion, tie and hold. The devil understands that the best way to hold a person back is through suggestions. Just simply ask Eve. Eve was brought to a seductive worldview through a simple suggestion. Satan packaged his theory with suggestions that would get the wheels turning in Eve's mind imploring to her that God is hiding something from her. After those thoughts tied itself around the truth in her heart, she and Adam was held out of Eden. One suggestion entertained led to the downfall of humanity. But thank God for the Seed Jesus that was planted amongst us that grew amongst us that dwelt amongst us and died for us allowing his fruit the Holy Spirit to fall to nourish us which now gives us the power to trample over any suggestion given to us to a now powerless enemy. You now have that power. Never communicate with a defeated foe. Communication with the enemy leads to destruction. He doesn't care if you are saved he cares if you are productive and the best way to stifle your productivity is to come through the cracked doors of your mind leaving suggestions that will try to gain root and hold you from your promised land. As long as the earth remains there will be seed time and harvest and suggestion ties and holds. Which one is thriving in your life now?

Take some time now to meditate on Philippians 4:4-9 and think about the importance of thinking on what is good. Once you have taken that time write down below both the good and bad thoughts that you are entertaining now and ask yourself why

Good Thoughts	Bad Thoughts	Why?

How a Stronghold Develops

A stronghold doesn't grow overnight – it grows over many nights. Night time can be a nightmare. The night time is the time of day many people regret or try to fill with unnecessary company due to the thoughts they are left with. Thoughts are one of Satan's most powerful tools of torment. He utilizes them to tangle us keeping us up at night and causing us to be foggy during the day. He wants our days to be draining.

Every stronghold begins as a seed. A cancerous seed. A seed designed to weaken our spiritual immune system. These seeds are the negative suggestions we discussed earlier. These seeds don't always come off as negative though, some of these suggestions make sense. Many of us are entertaining good advice but not God advice. All good advice is NOT God advice. A lot of people wish us well and desire to see us succeed, but not all their suggestions are God inspired. That's why it is important to know God for yourself and to be sensitive enough to know and obey his voice. A lot of people are still bound by "good advice". Good for them doesn't always mean good for you. This worlds system has created a warped perspective in a lot of people's minds causing them to think what's bad is good and what's good is bad. A lot of people suggest that sex outside of marriage is good, or that living with your girlfriend or boyfriend is wise or watching pornography is cool or that quitting their God dream to pursue a 6-figure job is ok. There are a lot of bad suggestions/ seeds sinking in the minds of a lot of people.

Before a negative seed is planted in your mind the enemy researches you to see what you will be more likely to receive. His demons don't waste time or resources, so they take their time to see what connects to you. They analyse your habits and your disciplines. They look through your history books to see how you was brought up and who abandoned you they look for loopholes in your contracts all to see where you are your weakest. So many of us work so hard to build our strengths that we overlook our weaknesses. Based on their research they will begin to set the stage for you to sink or soar beyond the safe limits of where God would like your emotions. He wants you to either sink into depression or soar into zeal and pride. He knows the power of your emotions that once you are high or low you will be receptive to just about anything tailored to you. Once you are in one of these states, a suggestion is made, planted quickly, hoping to change the way you see yourself, God, others and resources causing you to mismanage them. Once that seed is planted they will continue to supply your mind with doubts, disbelief or dangerous levels of high esteem, hoping to buy their seed, time to grow. Once the research has been made, and the seed has been planted and supplied for he then begins to lead you into building a soul tie to a fake saviour. See he wants anything and anyone to be your saviour instead of Jesus because he knows that anything outside of Jesus can only temporally save. Jesus is the only one that can eternally and completely save you. It's crazy how so many of us forfeit Jesus for frauds. These soul ties begin to grow over time eventually building strongholds. Imagine where you would be today if the seed that was planted in your mind at 6, 15 or 25 was uprooted? Imagine where you would be today if you would have listened to the Holy Spirits voice when he told you he or she wasn't it for you? Imagine how much time could have been devoted to your business if you would have followed your dreams instead of your moms or dads. One bad thought planted at the right time can waste a ton of years. Being soul tied to a person, place product or perspective will eventually turn into a stronghold a place in your mind where you can't pass. Our greatest barriers lie in our minds. What mental blockers are keeping you from progressing? Have you ever seen the meme of the horse tied to a lawn chair or the meme of the elephant tied to a stake in the ground? That's how many of us are we are physically active enough to be free but are too mentally weak to be free. You are only as strong as your mind.

Your enemy wants you to see your small thoughts as towers he wants you to see this patch of dingy grass as a forest. He wants you to be overwhelmed and wants you to feel as if this molehill in front of you is a mountain that you can't move. But those thoughts are only suggestions and if you knew who the senders were you would send them back because they only give half-truths. Just because what you see, hear or think is true doesn't mean its Gods truth and just because its true today doesn't mean it will be true tomorrow. He is the one capable of changing your life completely around. What is luring you today? What is latching onto you today? Is it worth the sleepless nights? Is it worth the tears in the morning? Only you can give thoughts power.

Take some time to do some research of your life and ask yourself what they could use in my life to have a reach into my life. Utilize the boxes below!

Your research	Their Reach in	What did you receive	Return to sender
What in your life could they use against you?	What did they use against you?	Did you accept what they used against you if so why?	What must you do to return what they sent back to them?

In order for these seeds to become strongholds, they need to be fed. Satan loves carnal appetites. He loves it when we no longer hunger and thirst after righteousness because he knows that we will seek elsewhere to be fed. This system is designed for you to awaken things in your life before its time. He wants you to have sex before its time, pursue companionship before its time he wants immature people to pursue mature things before the time. He knows that once you taste cool aid for the first time you will never want water again, and if you never want water again then you won't be properly hydrated. He wants you to replace what you need for something that will destroy you from the inside out. And that's what's been going on for years. One moment with pornography leads to masturbation and masturbation then leads to the need to add a partner then once the partner is no longer satisfying then it leads to multiple partners. Then once multiple partners can't suffice then that appetite leads to desiring the same sex; once the same sex then lord knows what else. See love awaken before its time turns into loves premature state; lust and lust has no boundaries. This process is in a lot of scenarios where one look at this or one conversation with this person or one listen to this leads to a series of actions leading to imprisonment. Satan wants you and me in cycles. When we are in cycles of self-sabotage, there is not much work required of His demons. They can then join forces to fight those that are disciplined. They don't waste time on those that are self-destructive but on those that are self-disciplined. Are you chasing the Christ and his character or are you still stuck in a sinful cycle?

Satan doesn't want you to have a soft hold but a stronghold. There is a difference. Based on your level of spiritual maturity or the renewing of your mind you can break free from soft holds. If someone has a soft hold on you and you are stronger than them, you can easily break free but if someone has a strong hold on you and they are stronger than you then you can't break free. Once we sin we are transferring our strength. Your enemy is after your energy. Your energy = your strength. If you try to execute on energy you don't have you will eventually experience burn out. That's what the enemy is after. He wants us to barter our energy for burn out. God is our ultimate source. When we are plugged into Him we never run out of energy or resources. Even when we are tired if we are working unto Him he will repay but when we are constantly giving over our energy into these pockets of sin, then we dilute our power. This system is an energy sucker. It uses porn, bad relationships, faulty family structures, cliques/ clubs, carnal/misguided support groups, media, music, etc. to drain us! Is your battery on 100% often or is it always on 3%? We are not mentally tired for no reason there is a reason why you are worn out mentally. If your mind is tired your senses become low. You will begin to forget who you are in Christ, who you are to yourself and who you are in society. In Christ you are strong but with Christ you learn how to use your strength. Stay with Christ and steward your energy. And don't let the enemy make a mountain out of a molehill, a patch of grass into a forest or a Lego building into a tower.

What are those thing that you are stronger than but is hindering you from going forward?

Not just what but why.

The questions I want you to focus on is not what you are tied to even though that is important but rather I want you to focus on why you are tied to it? The what is noticeable but the why not so much. In order to be free, you must find the seed of the situation or when it was conceived. Everything and I mean everything, except for God, has a beginning. Find the beginning, and you can find the path to freedom. For years we have been fighting the "what" instead of searching for the "why". You must go all the way back to when you were introduced to what you are soul-tied to now. See your enemy doesn't fight fair and takes every opportunity of vulnerability. He didn't tempt Jesus when he was about his father's business at 12 or when he was being baptized by John He was tempted when He was hungry and vulnerable in the wilderness. He always looks for a more opportune time where he can capitalize. He will take 10 minutes of vulnerability at 10 years old to ensure he has a ten-year hold. He doesn't want a 10-minute hold, or a 10-month hold he wants decades! Because not a lot can happen in 10 minutes or 10 months, but a lot can happen decades from now. Marriage can happen, having kids can happen, starting a ministry can happen, a death in the family can happen, and he wants his tree or trees to be in the middle of your yard, keeping you from being the husband or the wife God wants you to be or keeping you from being the father or mother God desires for you to be. Keeping you from being the minister, friend, co-worker God wants you to be. He wants you tied to a tree he planted instead of embracing what Christ did on a tree for you! He wants you to grow up with voids, with feelings of neglect and abandonment he wants you to feel betrayal he wants you to feel low so that he can fill you up with all kinds of suggestions that will turn into strongholds. It's hard to be victorious when you are vulnerable but never forget who won the victory over your vulnerabilities and who died so you can reclaim your dominance. You were created to have dominion not only over the birds of the air or the fish in the see but the thoughts that are flying and swimming in your mind right now. Kill what could be; by removing its seeds.

What soul ties/ strongholds are in your life right now?	When were they conceived?

What caused them to develop?	How are they affecting you as a man, woman, husband, wife, parent, minister, business owner etc.?

Healthy vs Unhealthy Soul-ties.

Let's take some time to discuss the differences between a healthy and an unhealthy soul tie. A healthy soul-tie is a proper, somewhat balanced connection with another person or thing. An unhealthy soul-tie is an improper unbalanced tie to a person or thing. All of us are tied to something the question is what kind of tie. There are 9 things we either have a proper/ healthy tie to that leads to stability or an improper/ unhealthy tie to that lead to a stronghold and they are;

1. People
2. Places
3. Products
4. Perspectives
5. Purpose & Passions
6. Power
7. The past and
8. The Person of God.

People

God created us to be communal beings. He designed us to be interdependent on each other, sharing ideas, perspectives, and support. The problem lies though in the effects of trauma, touch and trickery that often times happens between people. Whenever we experience trauma, touch or trickery in moments of vulnerability, a memory wrapped in a feeling is birthed. God designed for love, care, selflessness, empathy, and discernment to be the catalyses of our relationships but due to our fallen nature, we sometimes lose the ability to manage each other with these traits.

Let's break down the effects of each one starting with trauma. Trauma is a state of mind where a person is the most lost. This mindset is birthed out of a deeply disturbing experience that was unexpected such as a loss in the family, sexual or domestic abuse, etc. These moments are designed moments by our enemy to keep us in a state of panic and depression. The enemy knows the effects of trauma he knows the unfortunate feelings they birth, and his goal is for us to be forever connected to that experience or individual for the rest of our lives. His goal is to use the trauma to open a door in your mind where he can organically allow the natural effects of the experience to continuously plant seeds of thoughts that will eventually grow into multiple strongholds. He needs tangible things and experiences in order to build intangible mental ties. Right now, you can remember every negative traumatic experience you've ever had with a person and right now you either feel nothing, a lot or a little emotion about that experience. There are three emotions you are feeling right now you are either feeling negative, numb or new. In every negative encounter with a person, you will be led to one of two extremes either numb or new. Satan wants you numb God wants you made new. Numbness is a negative effect from a negative experience. Numbness means hardness and it is one of the final stages of bitterness. Being indifferent doesn't make you different in a good way it makes you stagnant. Many of us are still suffering from the effects of trauma. You can't change what happened, but you can change what happens from here. Have you forgiven that person? Have you let that experience go? Like I tell everyone it could have been worse; you could have died. If you are alive, then you survived! Let that traumatic experience go and forgive them so that God can use that traumatic experience to make you into a new person. God sees the positive in every negative situation. He allows things to happen or allows the consequences of our sins to take their duration because he can see ways those two can be used for our good. If you love God and have embraced his purpose for you, then you are guaranteed to be made new from these experiences (Rom 8:28), but if you are mad at God and/or still sinking in the effects of those experiences, then you will never know what it means to be free. When we don't forgive we allow a negative soul tie to build leading to a stronghold in our lives.

What traumatic experiences have you experienced in your life and how are they effecting you now?

In what ways could those traumatic experiences be used for your good now?

Touch!

Our largest organ is our skin. The skin has multiple functions it lets us know when we are cold and hot, it's a protective shield, and it lets us know when we have been touched. Touch is a powerful sense due to its ability to communicate with the mind. Every touch registers a category in our minds. It registers if the touch was good, dangerous, accepted, sexual, or inappropriate and it also attaches a person to the touch as well. A lot of us have been touched appropriately, sexually, and physically and within the right context are fine, but we all have, to some degree, experienced the negative effects of these touches. A lot of us have been betrayed by a touch. What we thought was a love touch was a touch filled with an agenda of lust. What we thought was an embrace was a lie. Satan knows the need we have for a touch and he knows the effects of not being touched and the effects of being overly touched. When a person grows up in a home where they have never been touched as far as embraced or cared for then that person will long to be touched, and when a person has been overly touched in a negative/ sexual way then that person too will be looking to be touched or to touch. Satan wants us all to long for a physical touch over a spiritual touch. When a person has been touched spiritually and has allowed that spiritual encounter to nurture their mind and soul then that person will build a discernment and an empathy that will guard them from being touched or to touch and will inspire them to touch the world. We all need a hug, a kiss, a playful push, sex (if married) we were built to need these things but whenever there is a deep need that need will lead to perversion. God warned us not to awaken things before their time he said this about love.

Whenever we awaken something prematurely, that mature thing will expose our immaturity. It will prove to us that we're incapable of managing it. It's crazy how tempted we are to touch things that say do not touch. I wonder why at times? Could it be that we want to see what happens once we touch it. Could it be that we want to relish in the power of choice and to do what we want or could it be we are just sinful people that want to break the rules. No matter what we think, the person who puts up the sign is the main person who knows why we shouldn't touch it. And instead of saying why not we should simply respect the individual's request. Sex, surplus, and certain seasons are not to be touched before their time. A good thing touched at the wrong time will always be dangerous. God cares about your maturity, and he cares about how you manage things because he knows the effects of being touched or touching prematurely. He knows that when you have sex with a person, your body will naturally register that this person is your husband or wife and will be the sole person to please you sexually and will log within your mind with your consent if it was a pleasurable or non-pleasurable experience. If it was pleasurable, it will now register this person as your mate. But imagine if you keep allowing yourself to be touched - you will confuse your body, and now natural comparisons will begin. That's why there are certain seasons to touch and to be touched because your body will register those experiences and those experiences will become memories that can't be erased.

But let me take some time to address those who didn't touch something prematurely but were touched inappropriately. A lot of people have been abused and touched inappropriately leading to significant strongholds. Some of you were raped, molested, domestically abused and you are now dealing with the effects of those moments. Some of you are privately struggling with your sexuality, struggling with living and some of you are thinking about ending your life. I want to encourage you that one touch from God can erase every negative touch from a man or a woman. See Satan wants you to embrace the pain of that negative embrace. He wants you to harbour resentment and un-forgiveness leading you to remain locked in your internal prison. But God wants to set you free. I know you have taken many showers trying to remove that sexual touch I know you beat your pillow at night due to what happened to you at your uncle or aunts house I know you are struggling but what Jesus felt from those Roman soldiers ripping his beard, hitting his face, stripping his flesh, spitting on his face, nailing his hands and feet and piercing his side was all done so that when you feel what you feel you can know he suffered beyond those moments so that you can trust him to help you endure. Satan wants you to continuously experience those negative touches over and over in your mind to fuel the resentment and insecurities in your heart buying time for those strongholds to take root and keep you bound. But what Jesus did for you is greater than what any person has done to you. God designed for us to have healthy ties to our spouses, children, and neighbours through touch but when we are not aware of the power of touch we will lead ourselves and possibly others down some dark paths.

What negative touches have you experienced and how are they affecting you now?

If you are still struggling with the effects of those touches take sometime below to talk/vent to God and let him minister to you.

Trickery.

It hurts deeply when we find out that we were tricked or betrayed by a person we trusted. Trust must be earned not freely given. Not everyone should have certain accesses to us and the depths a person goes in our lives should be audited by spiritual discernment to ensure that we and everything else connected to us is protected. Our trust should be delegated only by the leading of the Holy Spirit because he is the only one that knows a person's integrity and ability. See not everyone is bad but not everyone is capable. Sometimes we put our trust in good people that are not capable. But a lot of negative strongholds happen when we put our trust in people who from the beginning had bad intent. We've all been burned by someone but that doesn't mean we allow that moment to make us trust no one because in life you are going to have to trust someone and being closed off doesn't help. But what we must allow these moments to do is build our discernment and trust in the Holy Spirit of God.

What does a healthy tie to a person looks like?

A proper tie to a person is a natural tie given by and sustained by God. My goal is to always have a natural tie to my wife, children, extended family, friends and those I serve through ministry but that natural tie all boils down to my dependence on God. My level of maturity in him will determine the balance of my tie to them. It will determine how I lead my family and lead people it will determine how I handle being disappointed by them and how to handle being celebrated by them. We need to allow God's voice to be the loudest and the most obeyed. We will have an improper tie to anyone we place above God. If you place your spouse or your desire for one above God, then you will cause an unhealthy tie to birth because your desire for them will supersede your dependence on God. We need to always be dependent on God so that he can moment by moment show us when we are doing the most or not doing enough in our relationships. That's why it's important for you to wait on God to bring you your significant other because that person too will understand their desperate need for God and when they make a mistake or are not moving properly in the relationship they will heed to the directions of God. If they are dependent on God and you feel they are not moving quickly enough or are not serving you correctly, you will know That God will let them know.

That's why before you cast your care to your spouse or loved ones cast them on God. But if you are in a relationship with a person that is not connected to God like that, then you will have to really press for their salvation and depend on God even more on how to handle every situation with kindness and gentleness. God is the source of all relationships. No person can complete you only God can. Many people are allowing their desires for companionship, children, and friends to go above their love for God and in doing this they destroy themselves. A healthy tie to a person begins when a heart is tied to God and is willing to be led by His Spirit. Men you need to always remain dependent on God so that you won't place God-like expectations on your wife, children, friends, etc. Ladies you need to always be dependent on God so that you won't place God-like expectations on your husband, children family or friends. Never expect something from someone that you love that you first don't expect from yourself and secondly don't expect something from someone that God doesn't expect from them because when you do, you will put too much pressure on them.

Who are the people you are connected to?	Are you Properly or Improperly tied to them?

What must you do to create a proper tie to each person?

Places.

All of our positive and negative experiences happened in a place and depending on what happened in those places will determine our feelings when those places are revisited. Some of us have a negative or overly positive tie to places. We either avoid them or overly frequent them due to our desires. Right now, you can remember to a degree the colours of the walls, the colour of the carpet, the smell of the room and the paintings on the walls of every place you've experienced a significant negative or positive experience. Everything is used in the process of the imprisoning or the freeing of a person. We have allowed these moments to give too much power to the places these moments happened in. We either avoid them or spend too much money to visit them keeping us from being free. Why are you avoiding them? Why are you overly visiting them?

The answers to these questions will set you free. People may leave, but not all buildings do. A lot of us can't go back to that restaurant or city where we experienced that break up because of how bad it was. Now I understand and have experienced a few breakups in my day, but those moments shouldn't be still heavy on us years later. You should by the help of God still be able to travel to a city or visit a restaurant and not enter deep depression. Depression is proof that you aren't and wasn't dependent on God. The best way to have a proper tie to a place is to know our place in God, within our responsibilities, and within our communities. When we are more focused on being in these places we will have a proper tie to any place we have experienced hurt or extreme happiness. If we are in God no matter where we go, he will be there. He will help us see the moments that happened within these places correctly and will lead us to forgive and to use wisdom financially.

What are your favorite places to visit and why?	Do you have an improper tie to these places if so why?

What places have you experienced deep hurt?	Are you still effected by the memory of these places? If so why?

Products.

A lot of people are improperly tied to a product. We as consumers have allowed ourselves to be consumed by products. We have allowed our identity to be identified with emblems instead of the image of God. If you take some time to observe different people groups you will see their obsession with brands. They rather be branded with the image of something created than to be branded with the Image of Jesus. Right now, you are bearing an image, and you have to ask yourself am I bearing the image of God or the world? People become perversely tied to a product when they need acceptance. When someone is always looking to be accepted instead of embracing their acceptance in God, they will self-destruct. No product on this planet can heal your insecurities or fill those empty voids. It's crazy how many of us spend hundreds and thousands of dollars to keep up with the Jones; a family that doesn't exist. Brands like Jordan, Luis Vuitton, Mercedes, Bentley, Pandora, Tiffany's, and Michael Kors have become our idols determining our worth. Your worth is not in what was created but in the creator. Don't get me wrong there is nothing wrong with purchasing from these companies but make sure you are not selling a piece of your soul in the purchase.

A proper tie to a product whether purchased or handed down all boils down to our perspectives. As believers, we were purchased into the family of God with the intent that everything we purchase or receive is owned by God and can be used by God at any time. We through Christ were created to be distribution channels not hoarders or extreme brand consumers. He desires for us to only be attached to him and that in any moment we can let go of any product whether it be a car, money, clothes, etc. The strength of your tie is evident in how long it takes for you to let go of something when God ask you to. What are those things in your life, if God was to ask you to give away, would be hard to give away?

1
2
3
4
5
6
7

Because whatever you find the hardest to give away is the thing that has too much of a hold on you. We must never forget that God always replenishes what we let go for him. He said that anyone that forsakes mother father, children land etc for my sake would receive a return not just in the life to come but in this life as well (Mark 10:29-30). When we become too attached to anyone or anything we will have a hard time in letting it go or when we have too high of a desire for something we will steal or sell our souls to have a piece of that "happiness". Trust me anything or anyone you pursue without God will leave you disappointed and potentially depressed at the end. Don't give too much power to a product, or a brand to the point that you feel that you are nothing without it.

A way I challenge people in this area is to begin to trim down the areas of their obsessions. Meaning start giving away the things that you feel you can't give away. Start asking God who could I bless with my best and in the letting go you will find freedom.

What are you favourite brands or products?	Are you obsessed with these things or nah? If so why?

In what ways could being overly obsessed with these brands/products affect you, your family or your purpose?

Perspectives.

Each one of us have a viewpoint and our viewpoint is predicated on our level of maturity. Many people boast that they have a good viewpoint, but they are too low to see what's there. Your perspective is how you view or see what you see. It all boils down to the meaning you give a person, place or thing. The highest viewpoint or perspective is the one God holds. No other perspective or viewpoint comes close. No matter how high a person thinks, they are not at the highest point. God can see everything and can see in everyone. He is the only being that's omnipresent, omniscience and omnipotent and he has to be these things to execute a perfect pardon and a perfect judgement. His omnipresence's gives him the ability to be everywhere simultaneously. His omniscience gives him the ability to know every thought and every motive simultaneously. He is able to know if your good works have good intentions. His omnipotence gives him the ability to give power, take away power, execute pardons and judgements. I say all that to say that his perspectives are supreme and all of ours are flawed. That's why even the person who is low in class if they view things how God views them their perspectives are higher than a person who is in the highest class but doesn't adopt Gods views.

How do you see what you see and how does God want you to see what you see? Answer the questions in the boxes below.

How do you see you?	How does God see you?
How do you see the opposite sex? + Spouse	How does God want you to see the opposite sex? + your spouse
How do you see money?	How does God want you to see money?
How do you use time?	How does God want you to use time?
How do you see those that are different from you?	How does God want you to see/ treat those different from you?

Purpose and passion.

All of us have laid awake at night wondering and pondering about our purpose. The number one question that needs an answer is why am I here? So many people are completely unaware of what their purpose is. When we know our overall purpose we will be able to see the purpose of each day. I thank God almost every day that I know my purpose and that I have the right perspective on it. There was a time in my life when I was too attached to my purpose so much so that it affected my health and my relationships. I became to consume with it to the point that I was doing a disservice to those I was sent to serve. Throughout the last 3 or 4 years God has really allowed me to feel the consequences of being soul –tied to a cause and to a mission and for that I am thankful. Do I have a perfect balance no but am I aware yes. God desires for us to be balanced he wants us to have a cause but not a cause to have us. When you become overly attached to your purpose or a cause you will become a threat to those closest to you and you will neglect God, yourself and your loved ones. Deep down inside when we are overly attached to a cause we are really looking for self-worth. You and your purpose are not one. Your purpose is a huge part of you, but it is not all of you. We must not look at the umbrella (purpose) but everything that is up under it. Everything in your life to a degree helps you to accomplish your purpose, but not everything should be used to the point of burn out that you lose everyone including yourself. A proper tie to your purpose or your passion is evident when you are able;

1. to take a break from it to rest or spend time with family
2. to pace yourself
3. to trust God with it

The flip side to all of this is that many people are attached to a purpose or a passion that God never gave them. It's one thing to burnout pursuing your God-given purpose but it is another thing to burn out pursuing another purpose. The enemy loves the effects of both he wants you at one of two extremes and never balanced. God has created you for such a time as this to utilize that time to produce what he has placed in you. He wants you to have the right perspectives with your purpose he wants you to always seek balance never overlooking what's most important. A lot of us overlook what's most important. In every situation that we face there is something that is most important and should rewire our attention. When a person's mind is not renewed things become out of place. God cares about our priorities, and he cares about how in-tune we are to him. The Holy Spirits job is to lead and to govern. He is here to help us see everything how they were supposed to be seen. He will let you know when you should dedicate time to your business and when to dedicate time to your family. He will help you avoid burnout and pursue balance. God wants you balanced; Satan wants you burned out. Look at your life right now are you balanced or are you burning out? Where in your life could you use a little more balance? Pursuing your purpose without patience and the proper perspectives will always lead you to powerlessness. What is causing you to love your purpose more than the one who gave it to you? There is nothing wrong with being passionate but make sure is balanced.

Honestly rank who/ what's most important to you right now and the time you commit to it daily or weekly.	
1	Time
2	Time
3	Time
4	Time
5	Time
6	Time
7	Time
8	Time
9	Time
10	Time

Based on the times above write below from most to least the things you commit your time to. This will show you what matters most to you.
1
2
3
4
5
6
7
8
9
10

Balanced or Burned out: write down below the areas you are experiencing burnout and the ways you can seek balance in that area.
Where are you experiencing burnout and why?

How can you seek balance in that area?

Power

Power without maturity is dangerous. To a degree all of us have power and our level of maturity will determine how we manage that power. A lot of people in our world lust for power. Their lust is infused with the need to prove their dominance, to prove their intellect etc. They only want power for praise and not for the promotion or the elevation of others. God wants us to use our power to serve others not to suppress them. Our world today is run by men and women whose whole objective is to hurt others with their power that with one stroke of a pen laws can be created to isolate them but endanger others. The beautiful thing about all of this is that Jesus is the supreme judge and will in due time execute his power over those that are mismanaging theirs. But for the believers, God cares about how you manage your power. God gives power to the prudent Satan gives power to the proud. The results of our world today lies in the hands of those in power. The most powerful person on this planet is not the ones who can move laws into place but those that can move heaven through prayer. Oh, if only God's people knew how much power they had and how powerful prayer and faith is... if we did we would be changing our worlds. But many of us care more about being promoted by man than we do by God. God promotes based on maturity and he promotes those whom he knows will do the right thing even when pressed. He gives power to those he knows that when tempted will remain disciplined. He looks for people who love him more than anything and will remain close to him to receive instructions. When you lack these things don't expect to be promoted by God. All of us have a superpower and our superpowers lie within our purpose anchored in the presence of God. Once a believer leaves the presence of God their power will be used to hurt and not heal.

What are your superpowers?	Who can benefit from them?	How should you manage them?	What is your superhero name?

A person that has a proper tie to their power is a person that truly loves people and seeks the best for them. Their fear for God leads them to reverence the dignity in others. They seek wisdom not wealth they are not drunk with power they are sober with it and they have the ability to discern what is best. They honour the power over them and they execute power gently under them. They treat those above them and those under them the same. See we must understand that God cares more about how we treat those underneath our power than he does those above it. God cares about how you treat your employees, your helpers in your ministry and everyone in service to you. He cares about your attitude towards those underneath, He cares about your attitude with people like the waiter, the bellman, the uber drive and the homeless he cares about them all. He cares about how you treat the least of these and if you are out there using your power recklessly and without honour then when the king of kings and the lord of lords calls your name we will see how you act under his power. Your level of reverence towards God will determine your reverence towards others. Don't drive drunk with power, use power responsibly.

The Past

The past was never meant to be a place of residence but a place of reference. So many people live more in their past then they do in their present. Being attached to your past will keep you from unwrapping the present. Many of us have hundreds of boxes or days that haven't been unwrapped. The best way for Satan to steal your present is to always present your past. There is nothing in yesterday that you can change it is cemented and can only be used for a reference. Your past was not meant to be a morgue but a museum. When I look back I don't see death I see growth. Your perspectives of your past will determine your perspectives on your future. Your past should be a museum where you see history, growth, maturity and distance, not death and destruction. Life is all about wins and lessons not wins and losses. We have allowed our mistakes to be stakes in the ground with ropes around them tied to our waist keeping us from progressing. When a person is improperly tied to their past they will become identified by it. They will always see themselves as a failure, as no good. See the past is truth past tensed just because it was true back then doesn't mean it will be true going forward. It's crazy what a little change would do.

Once you change your perspectives on your past you will be prepped to be pushed into a promising future. A person who is properly tied to their past sees only two things significant back there and that's the cross Jesus died on and the cross they denied their life to pick up. Everything else are lessons. I used to be so attached to what happened in my life and who left that it kept me from honouring and loving on those that stayed. I began to recycle old emotions into new situations causing the same cycles to form but when I realised that I couldn't change the past or the minds of those in my past I began to really cherish the moment. See every moment matters. If only we took every moment seriously how bright would our past be? What you do today will determine what's in your past tomorrow. You may not be able to control what others do to you, but you sure can control what you do. Make your past brighter!

What significantly happened in your past? (Good and Bad)	How do you see these moments and how do they affect you now?	How should you see these moments?

The person of God.

Now I know what you're thinking You're like how is it possible to have an improper tie to God? Trust me it is possible. An improper tie to God is evident with a person who studies but never applies. They are attached to the idea of God and not God himself. They are puffed up with their knowledge of theology and have won the perfect attendance award in going to church, but when you look deeply into their lives there is no evidence of application. God wants us to be interdependent on him meaning he doesn't want us to be overly dependent on him or insufficiently dependent on him. An interdependent person 100% depends on God for their salvation but doesn't necessary depend on him for every minute thing. They know how to work independently from him. They know how to take what was given to them during their private time with God and implement it during their public life. A person who is overly dependent on God is a person who wants God to do literally everything. They won't do anything without him to a degree that's wisdom but not when he has told you to do something. God only goes halfway with us most of time. The only time God fully went all the way was through his son Jesus any other time he wants us to contribute. Everything that is created is half of an equation meaning it was created to do some of the work but not all. Even if it does all the work (like something purchased from a store) it still requires you to go to the store to purchase it, to plug it up etc. God wants you to do something not watch him do everything. A proper tie to God is a complete dependence on him for the saving of our souls and some dependence in producing solutions. Everyone on the planet falls into one of these categories they are either overly dependent, interdependent or not dependent at all which one are you?

The 3 strengths of a tie

Let's take some time now to talk about the three different strengths of a tie. There are weak ties, mild ties and strong soul ties, and each of these have the potential to produce strongholds. A weak tie is a tie that is not strong at all, maybe the tie is at its early stages or certain thoughts may have just crossed your mind. A weak tie is a tie that at any moment you can break from it. These ties may represent something you may have touched once or has briefly caught your interest but hasn't caught root.

A mild tie is a tie where there seems to be a little tug. You are beginning to become emotionally and mentally invested and the thoughts are moving in. Subtle actions begin to affect you, meaning that whatever has caught your interest now has a subtle tug on you to the point that one small action somewhat affects you.

The subtle things like - he doesn't call as much as he used to, she doesn't pay you that much attention like she used to, you are no longer favoured on your job like you used to be. These actions begin to affect you and you begin to feel a certain way about what you are interested in. Whenever you feel a certain type of way about something, you are experiencing a mild tie.

A strong tie is a connection to something/ someone you feel you just cannot live without! At the simple mention of a person, you become sick, depressed or hard-hearted, or too elated and overjoyed. This thing affects your mood and your movements meaning you are on a somewhat never-ending roller coaster of emotions. With a strong tie there is no middle ground meaning the person, place or thing will have you swinging from either extremely happy or extremely depressed. The mild tie, you may find yourself in the middle ground at times, a weak tie you may find yourself in the middle ground at times, but a strong tie has you at severe extremes. There is nothing wrong with being sad, happy or frustrated about a situation but when that thing or person makes you happier than God can or makes you depressed then that thing has too much of an hold in your life. Idolatry is where all sins find their roots. You've got to ask yourself, "Why am I so invested? Why am I so tied to this person?"

What do you have a weak tie to?	What do you have a mild tie to?	What do you have a strong tie to?

Spiritual, emotional, mental and physical ties.

Let's talk about spiritual, emotional, mental and physical ties. Strongholds aim to connect their roots and to build restriction to each area of your being.

Let's talk about spiritual soul ties and strongholds. The core of a spiritual stronghold are the following

1. Church hurt,
2. False teaching,
3. false expectations,
4. Idolizing a spiritual leader.

Church Hurt

A negative spiritual tie or stronghold can begin through being hurt through the church. Many people right now are mad at God because of what happened in a church. I tell people you never judge a faith by its followers, you judge it by the one who established the faith. We were never supposed to put all of our trust into people we were supposed to put our trust in God. People no matter how good their intentions are will hurt you but God will never hurt you. Being church hurt is not a valid reason for you to be tied to another way of life, tied to another religion, or tied to something else. It's sad that many people have allowed church hurt to keep them from being healed by a good God and a solid/ healthy fellowship. If you are experiencing the effects of church hurt hurry to the arms of God through your private relationship with Him and let him heal you, strengthen you and lead you to healthy fellowship.

False Teaching

False teaching is another thing that causes spiritual soul ties and strongholds. Many people are now spiritually tied to false teaching due to laziness or emotionalism. It is our responsibility to know what we believe, it is our responsibility to find truth and to make sure truth is applied in every part of our lives. There are no excuses for anyone to follow false teachings if they are truly being led by the Teacher. Our main fellowship should be with the Holy Spirit whose main objectives are to lead us to God's word, point us to Jesus, and lead us under teachings that will aid in His work in our lives. Our source for teaching should begin inward then outward and it should always stem from a faithful commitment to the scriptures and the leading of the Holy Spirit.

False Expectations

Many people become spiritually souled tied to certain things due to false expectations, or when God doesn't meet their carnal expectations. God is not obligated to meet our carnal expectations He is not a stubborn God but a settled God a God that cannot contradict His character. A lot of people leave God due to their false expectations. They leave the true God to create one that will meet their expectations. When a person does this, they will become tied to false teachings and false leaders that will lead them into great danger.

Idolizing a Spiritual leader.

Satan has created a culture within the church that idolizes its spiritual leaders, having people worship the pastor more than they worship God. Often times people end up becoming spiritually connected to the ones that led them to Christ or discipled them under the name of Christ. God never intended for these individuals to be the sole source of your spiritual consumption he didn't call them gods he called them gifts. Those who are leaders within the body of Christ are gifts given by God to establish, redirect, reach, Shepard and teach the body. The problem lies in the insecurities and evil intent of some of our leaders. Many people desire these positions to establish their cults hoping to be surrounded by individuals that will worship them instead of God. The best meals are the meals that are cooked at home. God wants your spiritual walk to consist mostly of your private worship than your public worship. If you find yourself eating out more so that eating at home, you could be in threat of idolizing a spiritual leader.

Mental soul ties or strongholds.

Whatever occupies your mind will determine how you move. There is a direct correlation between your mind and your movements. Wherever your mind is sitting right now your life will soon take a seat next to it. Your life will soon mirror the quality of your thoughts. What is the quality of your mind? Do you have a healthy mind or an unhealthy one? The enemy understands the importance of tying your mind to destructive thoughts. He wants your mind to be tied to depression, suicide, lust, death, envy he wants you to allow these weeds to take root keeping you from growing fruit. You are a direct reflection of your thoughts.

I have his formula that will shed some light on how mental soul-ties are formed.

- Significant moments will lead to significant memories.
- Significant memories will lead to significant momentum,
- Significant momentum will lead to significant movements.

Right now, you can remember every significant moment you had in your life. You can remember your darkest moments as well as the brightest. Satan has designed a system aimed at ensuring you have significant highs and significant lows. He knows that you can never forget what was significant. He wants you always to be led by insignificance into moments that you will always remember. The more intense the moment the less likely you will forget it. He knows that if I can get you to indulge in a moment that you are not mature enough to handle, then he can at any moment use it against you in the future. One of his greatest weapons are memories. A memory is just a saved moment. A moment you will never forget. That's why he goes through great measures to get you to have your first when you are the most immature like for instance sex. Everyone who has had sex remembers there first and remembers just about everyone they have had sex with. This plays a part in hindering people from experiencing true love. Marriage is not sustained by sex its sustained by God and friendship. Sex was meant to be expressed after God, after friendship, and after marriage; never before. Once a person has sex outside of the context of a marriage submitted to God they now awaken an appetite for sex. Everyone knows that it is hard to come back from being sexually triggered. Being sexually triggered leads to sexual seasons and sexual seasons leads to sexual consequences. Satan loves for us to be burdened with consequences and condemnation and the best way to ensure that, is to use our memories to birth significant momentum meaning heighten emotions that will lead us to continue to make the same moves. Demons don't waste their time on people that are trapped in cycles they just let their appetites control them. They want you mentally tied to an addiction to the point that it becomes a stronghold. It doesn't matter what your intentions are if you still silently struggle with a memory you will only repeat them. Is your memory bank full of treasure or torment?

Listen, there is one significant moment that should change how you think, and that's the moment when Jesus sat at the right hand of the Father. That significant moment should change the way you move and how you remember. Satan wants your mind and your heart to work separately. God never intended for your brain and your heart to work independently of each other, he wanted them to work together. God gave you a mind to guard your heart. Many of us have our minds on ice and our hearts on flame and we do whatever we feel. When you do whatever you feel you begin to feel on things prematurely and dig yourself into things that will only cause your ties to become stronger.

What is in your memory bank? Write down below the treasures and/or torments that are in your mind right now and write down how you can see your significant moments differently.

Treasures	Torments

How can you change the way you remember your negative significant moments?

Physical ties.

Satan understands the power of our senses. He understands that when a person engages in touch, hunger, thirst, or, in any other form of our basic needs then our bodies will become attached. That is why in order to break a soul tie or stronghold you've got to break it in each compartment. Most people think, "Oh, if I repent and believe and pray then it is broken everywhere." No, no, no. Things have been broken in the spirit realm but you have to cooperate with the sanctification process of Christ in order for God to break the emotional, mental and physical holds because whenever a person engages with forbidden things or things out of season those things will cause biological, mental and emotional effects.

Let's now discuss some scriptures on strongholds and soul ties and how we are supposed to handle them. There are two scriptures we are going to talk about right now in this book - 2 Corinthians 10:3-4 and Ephesians 6:10-17.

Let's look at 2 Corinthians 10:3-6, *³ For though we walk in the flesh, we are not waging war according to the flesh. ⁴ For the weapons of our warfare are not of the flesh but have divine power to destroy strongholds. ⁵ We destroy arguments and every lofty opinion raised against the knowledge of God, and take every thought captive to obey Christ, ⁶ being ready to punish every disobedience, when your obedience is complete.*

There are four things this scripture tells us, it tells us 1) that there is no help in the flesh, 2) there is no help in carnal weaponry, 3) you destroy arguments through knowing God's point of view and 4) we must take every negative thought captive to obey Christ.

Let's look at the first verse - *For though we walk in the flesh we are not waging war according to the flesh.* Many people confuse themselves into thinking that they can fight a spiritual battle through natural means. You can't endeavour to win a spiritual battle using natural resources like hands, feet, etc. We have to use spiritual weaponry, this is a spiritual battle, and we need to be walking in the spirit in order to win. This natural world is only a reflection of the spiritual world meaning the spiritual world is bigger and is the cause to the effects that happen in the natural. We must always remember that we are spiritual beings first not second or third.

This is a spiritual battle and in order for us to win, we have to walk in the spirit. We cannot face or fight a spiritual battle spiritually unclean. You have to make sure that you allow the sanctification process of God to purge you, to cleanse you. That is why I always say in my videos, is the Holy Spirit too busy cleaning you than he is using you? Is he too busy cleaning the same window day after day after day, the same walls day after day or is he excited to use you? Are you useful or useless?

Let's go to verse four - F*or the weapons of our warfare are not of the flesh or carnal but have divine powers to destroy strongholds.* To defeat demons, our weaponry must be divine. Divine power comes from and is increased by our complete dependence and dedication to God. In order to defeat them we have to build our strength in God. You cannot overcome a porn addiction, a sex addiction, a lying addiction, a greed addiction without divine power. We have power through Christ to defeat any demonic stronghold. But if you are unaware of your weaponry and what type of divine power it has, you won't be able to destroy your strongholds. To destroy Satan's kingdom in your life, your neighbourhood, your relationship, your job, you must first destroy your strongholds; first things first. Whatever that is dark in you will be used against you in warfare. You have to take care of you first before you endeavour to go after the things of God, because if you are not stable, if you are not whole you will not be useful.

What are our spiritual weapons? Our spiritual weapons are

1. Fasting
2. Prayer
3. Accountability
4. Confession
5. Obedience
6. Meditation

Fasting:

Fasting has become a lost art form. Fasting is the recognizing of poor spiritual performance and restricting the flesh and the soul of its desires to bring one back into focus and success with God. A lot of people fast improperly. They fast to get an answer vs. fasting to get closer to the Answer who is God. Revelation comes through relationship. The closer you are to God the more He reveals. Fasting must be a tool used through obedience to God and through self-awareness. God knows everything including what's ahead and will lead us into individual fast or corporate fast to fasten us into position for what's ahead. Fasting through self-awareness is you fasting due to you noticing poor performance in your life. Most of our spiritual performance is due to what we consume spiritually, emotionally and physically. When we clog ourselves with impurities daily, weekly and monthly our spiritual performance declines. Just like with a vacuum or with a car when certain filters are clogged and not clean it affects the overall performance of the instrument. Those that are spiritually mature can recognize when they are not operating at a high level and will initiate a fast to get themselves back into peak performance. Fasting cannot not be used as a gimmick to try and "force" God into telling us what our carnal heart wants to know but it must be a tool used out of immense love for God desiring to be closer to him. When this weapon is used correctly, it will cause a ton of damage to the kingdom of Satan because you are rejuvenated and ready for the battle. Revelation is revealed through relationship. God doesn't yell he often whispers so that only those closest to him will hear him.

Prayer

Prayer like fasting is essential in getting things done and defeating the enemy. Any relationship that lacks communication is destined to fail. Communication is the glue that keeps a relationship thriving. The same is with God. The lack of communication with God doesn't affect God it drastically affects us. He is the one with the play by play intel for our lives and everything and everyone connected to us. No prayer No power, no prayer no protection, no prayer no peace. God wants to communicate with us and he wants to tell us the specifics. Like when God was speaking to Ananias in Acts 9:10-19 the bible reads;

10 Now there was a disciple at Damascus named Ananias. The Lord said to him in a vision, "Ananias." And he said, "Here I am, Lord." 11 And the Lord said to him, "Rise and go to the street called Straight, and at the house of Judas look for a man of Tarsus named Saul, for behold, he is praying, 12 and he has seen in a vision a man named Ananias come in and lay his hands on him so that he might regain his sight." 13 But Ananias answered, "Lord, I have heard from many about this man, how much evil he has done to your saints at Jerusalem. 14 And here he has authority from the chief priests to bind all who call on your name." 15 But the Lord said to him, "Go, for he is a chosen instrument of mine to carry my name before the Gentiles and kings and the children of Israel. 16 For I will show him how much he must suffer for the sake of my name." 17 So Ananias departed and entered the house. And laying his hands on him, he said, "Brother Saul, the Lord Jesus who appeared to you on the road by which you came has sent me so that you may regain your sight and be filled with the Holy Spirit." 18 And immediately something like scales fell from his eyes, and he regained his sight. Then he rose and was baptized; 19 and taking food, he was strengthened.

There is a lot of nuggets in this text Let's start with verse 10 where it says that there was a disciple at Damascus named Ananias,

God trust those that are deep in the discipleship process. A disciple is one who is disciplined under the teachings of Jesus. God knew He could trust Ananias due to his response. Ananias immediately said when his name was called once "Here I am Lord". Notice the bible doesn't say that God had to call him 3 or 4 times it just said once. God trust those that are readily available. He also said lord-signifying submission. God loves to dialogue with those that are present and that respect Him as lord meaning provider, overseer master, etc. God was also extremely detailed about when, where, how, and who. I share all this to say when you honour God and are readily available he will give you all the details you will need from the location, the name and what they will be doing when you get there. Imagine where we would be today if we were this close to God? Imagine how easy it would be to defeat Satan in every area of our lives with God giving us details like this. But if it takes God more than once to say your name for you to respond then its proof you are not that close. Prayer is a dialogue with God its always having the phone on; it's always being ready to obey even if we don't understand. Going to God should not be reserved for bad times we should always want to talk to God even randomly. What an opportunity we have to be able to talk with God anytime, it is just sad most choose not to.

Accountability

Some people may not see accountability as a weapon, but it is. Accountability leads to sustainability. With the right kind of accountability, we can accomplish anything with the right level of maturity. All of us need a personal accountant to ensure that we are adequately managed. Sin thrives where there is no accountability. Where in your life do you lack accountability? Wherever that place is you are vulnerable. I'm not saying you need 50 people you just need a solid small group of people who are saved, seasoned and secure. Meaning they are in love with God and understand grace, they are seasoned meaning they are familiar with the different stages of walking with God and they are not gossipers. You need people who have free access to your dark and vulnerable areas helping you to grow. The problem with accountability is that people don't want it due to their love for their sin. If you love God more than your sins, you will without tire seek for accountability.

Who are your accountants and in what areas are they holding you accountable?

Accountants	Areas

If you don't have any accountability write down below the areas you know you need accountability and pray to God to send you people and when he does write their names beside the areas.

Areas	Accountants & Date added

Confession

1 John 1:9 If we confess our sins, he is faithful and just to forgive us our sins and to cleanse us from all unrighteousness.

James 5:16 Therefore, confess your sins to one another and pray for one another, that you may be healed. The prayer of a righteous person has great power as it is working.

Proverbs 28:13 Whoever conceals his transgressions will not prosper, but he who confesses and forsakes them will obtain mercy.

These three scriptures show us the benefit of confessing our sins it says that if we confess we will

- Be forgiven and cleansed from all unrighteousness
- Be healed and
- Obtain mercy

It's hard to follow God with the weight of condemnation on us and with the feelings of unworthiness. Confessing our sins should not be embarrassing but edifying knowing that God will forgive, forget and remain faithful to us like he was faithful to Jesus. The scriptures above let us know the benefits of confessing our sins and the burdens of not confessing them. It says in 1 John that God is faithful to forgive us and cleanse us from all unrighteousness; keyword all. We must ask the Holy Spirit of God to reveal to us our unrepentant sin. A lot of us are suffering due to unrepentant sin. Unrepentant sin will still have residual effects on a believer's life years after their confession. True confession comes from a deep despair over one's sin, a deep understanding of the sins effects on them and those connected to them and from a deep love for God. Not all confessions are honoured by God we must confess deeply and truly.

For us to confess our sins confidently, we must be in a community where confession and accountability is a way of life. Confession is not safe in all communities. Some Christian communities are designed to be country clubs and clichés, and usually, those places breed gossip. For the healing in James 5 to work there must be a safe culture and community for each of us to confess to.

Proverbs 28:13 warns us about what happens when we conceal our confessions. It's hard to truly prosper with unconfessed sin. You may make a lot of money, but that anger, lust, pride etc. in your heart will rob you eventually of your success. But when we confess and not forsake them we will obtain mercy. You can't still mix and mingle in your sin and expect mercy you must forsake them for the mercy of God to cover you.

What shallow or deep sins do you need to confess to God now.

1	
2	
3	
4	
5	
6	
7	

Obedience

If you truly want to be safe, stay in the middle of of Gods will. Im sure you've heard the old saying "the will of God won't lead you where the grace of God can't keep you. The enemy can't do anything to you when you are in the will of God. That's why they wait for you to get comfortable to try and lure you out of obedience. Obedience is a fruit of reliance and reverence. Many of us don't obey God due to a lack of trust and due to arrogance. We can't see what God can see. Why put your trust in your tunnel vision when God in one glace can see your past, present, and predestined future.

Obedience is better than sacrifice.

I'm sure you have heard of the story in the bible where Saul one of the kings of Israel disobeyed God in the killing of all the livestock and the Amalekites. He instead brought back the best of the spoils. He in his opinion thought that it would be a great gift to God. He thought his worship would cover him from being judged for disobeying God. It was at that moment when the prophet Samael denounced him as king over Israel telling him that God was no longer with him. Complete obedience is the greatest form of worship. Partial obedience is 100%

disobedience. Every detail matters to God one slip could cause harm to you or anything connected to you. That is why it's is extremely important for us to trust God. Demons gain an entrance into our lives when we disobey God. Jesus said if you love me you will keep my commandments. It's hard to keep anything that you don't love that's why its important for God to be our ultimate love because whoever you love the most you will keep their commands. How much do you love God? The proof is in your obedience.

Meditation

Meditation is not memorizing scripture its marinating in the scriptures. Memorizing scripture is cool but if you are not abiding by it then it won't be effective for you. The enemy is not concerned about you knowing scriptures they are concerned when you become the scriptures. Becoming the scripture means you know it, you believe it and nothing can convince you otherwise. That when you are faced with fear, you become faith that when you are faced with lust you become love. You combat the contradiction of scripture by embodying the character of the scripture, and that doesn't happen overnight it happens over time. Your level of faithfulness is predicated on your level of fellowship. You can't defeat a full-time devil putting in part-time work. You have to be relentless in hiding God's word in your heart that you might not sin against him. The bible can't just always reside on your shelf it must reside in your heart that within any moment of temptation you are able to go in the satchel of your heart and pull out a scripture in faith. Memorizing scripture is half the battle you have to be so marinade in it that you speak it in faith. Chicken by itself is bland but when it sits in a marinade overnight all of a sudden, it becomes the flavour of the marinade. Whatever you soak in you will become. Right now, do you know 5 scriptures on lust to combat lust? Do you know 5 scriptures off the top of the dome on pride to combat pride? This war is too serious not to have the right words to fire back in faith. You have to spend time with your bible and really refine your understanding and usage of them so that every day you are ready to fight.

Write down below 1 to 3 things you are fighting right now and under them write down scriptures you can marinade in to use in battle when tested again. Simply go to google and type in scriptures on _____ (whatever you are facing) and you will be able to find a list of scriptures my favourite website for this is openbible.info.

Area 1 →
Scripture 1
Scripture 2
Scripture 3

Area 2 →
Scripture 1
Scripture 2
Scripture 3

Area 3 →
Scripture 1
Scripture 2
Scripture 3

Let's continue

Verse five - *We destroy arguments and every lofty opinion raised against the knowledge of God and take every thought captive to obey Christ.* There is a big difference between vain and valid imaginations. Vain by definition means pointless; valid by definition means something that has a point. When a person entertains vain imaginations or vain arguments, then that person is unaware of just how pointless that argument is. The Holy Spirit must be our filter. The Bible says we transform by the renewing of our minds, that there has to be something processing our thoughts as we receive them. If we don't have the right filter we will allow mercury; we will allow fluoride and other things to creep through our water hindering us from growing. You've got to ask yourself, "Do I have the right filter? Am I willing to make sure that I process every thought before it gets in there?" That is why you have to change how you think in order to filter what you think.

All strongholds begin as arguments, lofty opinions and suggestions. There is nothing smaller than a thought; think about that. Everything that we have faced, every stronghold that we had/have; began as a thought. We don't argue with Satan, we execute our authority over Satan and his demons. You and your mind cannot defeat the arguments of Satan, you in your own strength cannot defeat his arguments. We are not smart enough to defeat his arguments, because he is brighter than us, smarter than us, wiser than us, he's been on this Earth longer than we have. We in our own minds and our own strength cannot defeat Satan. But when you allow the spirit of God to lead you, and you begin to be dependent on his discernment and his ability to see things beyond the natural eye, then you become effective. But most people entertain these arguments, these lofty opinions and they begin to argue with Satan and they forget that Satan has seen their kind before. He knows how to get you right back into that sex bed; he knows exactly how to get you right back angry with your mom, he knows exactly what to do to get you right back at square one with your sins. However, if you execute in your authority in Christ, you through your knowledge, prayer, fasting and your spiritual disciplines will be strong enough to combat those arguments.

You do not combat Satan's arguments with arguing; you combat them with the word of God. When Jesus was tempted in the wilderness three times he did not engage in debates with Satan; the situation didn't last hours upon hours or days upon days. He completely responded with what he was full of, and since he was full of the Word, he responded with the word of God. He will always, Satan, present opinions that seem higher than the commands of God; that's why they call them lofty opinions. He will always present opinions that seem higher; things seem higher when you don't know the highest. He will always present opinions that make you feel like, "Man, this might be bigger and better than what God has told me." But they end up being less. You must know the loftiest point of what you are going through to defeat Satan's highest opinion. The loftiest point is the King of kings, the Lord of lords, the God of all gods, he is the loftiest, and his loftiest point is in his Word - his loftiest point on money, his loftiest point on sexuality, his loftiest point on praying or whatever it is, is in his word. You've got to make sure that you consult and know his loftiest point about whatever you hear, because it will always trump Satan's highest opinion; that's why they call God the Most High.

You must know God to receive and execute in his wisdom and knowledge. It is in us knowing him and loving him that we receive our power. Listen, you have to be connected, and God is not just going to connect to anyone. When you truly love him, you embrace him, and you care about everything that he cares about, and you will begin to receive his power. I always have this saying 'no prayer no power, some prayer some power, a lot of prayer a lot of power.' My question to you is, how much power do you have? It is our responsibility to take every thought captive to obey Christ. The more we entertain a thought that is not of God the more it proves we are either not knowledgeable in that area or we are unwilling to find out what God really says.

Our enemy preys on our ignorance and he preys when we do not pray. He understands that the less I can get you to talk to God the more vulnerable you will become. That's why it is your responsibility to take every thought that comes to your mind that is negative captive. You have to be able to take that thought captive, you have to grab it, put cuffs on it, bring it to the interrogating room and process that thing with Christ and his knowledge. Every negative thought must be arrested immediately; any thought you give time to; is a thought that will be used against you. The longer you let that thought live in your mind the quicker it will become a stronghold.

Verse 6 says - *Being ready to punish every disobedience when your obedience is complete.* In order for me to punish disobedience, I must be in complete obedience. It is going to be real hard to punish a thought if you are disobedient in an area. Disobedience in any area of your life will open the door to the enemy to invade. In order for me to punish disobedience, I must be prepared in obedience. Obeying God is training. The route God is leading you down is full of modules and experiences to help you see how to handle what life has a head of you. Not practicing obedience now will cripple you when you really need to be obedient in the future. People look at obeying God as a chore or as an "I'll only do it if you _____" treating God as if he will have to pay us back. The price it cost Jesus to redeem us encompasses the full total of us obeying God a million times. He owes us nothing. I must practice knowing and obeying his voice now so that when it is important for me to obey I will. How quick do you obey? Are you a Mr/Mrs. Immediately or a Mr/ Mrs. Eventually?

What negative thoughts are you fighting now and why?	What does the word of God say about each negative thought?	What systems are you going to put in place to arrest these thoughts?

***

Now let's look at Ephesians 6:10-17. Some of the points that I am going to share are in my book World War Me I'm only going to go over these points briefly but if you would like to read more on what I have to say about spiritual warfare feel free to get my book on Amazon today.

Finally, be strong in the Lord and in the strength of his might. Put on the whole armour of God that you may be able to stand against the schemes of the devil. For we do not wrestle against flesh and blood but against the rulers, against the authorities, against the cosmic powers over this present darkness, against the spiritual force of evil in the heavily places. Therefore, take up the whole armour of God that you may be able to withstand in the evil day, and having done all, to stand firm. Stand therefore, having fastened on the belt of truth and having put on the breastplate a righteousness, and, as shoes for your feet, having put on the readiness given by the gospel of peace. In all circumstances take up the shield of faith with which you can extinguish all the flaming darts of the evil one, and take the helmet of salvation, and the sword of spirit which is the Word of God.

Let's look at the first verse - *Finally be strong in the Lord and in the strength or the power of his might.* God's strength is made perfect in our weakness or in other words, his strength becomes proven when we acknowledge our weaknesses. Weakness here doesn't mean that I'm unable to lift something or that I'm physically weak, it just means that I am incapable in my own strength to succeed completely at anything without God. So, in order for me to be strengthened and encouraged to press forward and to fight against any type of demonic attacks, I must make sure that my strength is given by God through the acknowledgement of my weakness. When we acknowledge that we are weak we become strong. The first step in gaining strength is acknowledgement, when I acknowledge that I am weak, that's when God can trust me with strength. God cannot trust His strength with people who in their own effort think they're strong. God can only trust you with strength when you first acknowledge how weak you really are compared to his actual strength. God is looking for people who can steward his strength, but you cannot steward his strength without humility.

This verse shows us where we can find our strength after acknowledgement. It says that we can find it in the Lord and in his might. Christ is the only Lord that can truly sustain us. His presence is like a fitness facility meaning that in order for me to build my strength I have to be trained in him. The price Jesus paid for me granted me a lifetime membership in the presence of the Father where I can be trained by the Holy Spirit for my purpose. His might represents his methods. His training methods like meditating on his word, fasting, praying and community will open us up to a reservoir of might to conquer any attack of the enemy. It sad how so many people have a lifetime membership to Heaven Fitness but never go into the gym. Whoever is your lord is your trainer and whoever is training you will determine the strength you will have. Are you allowing the Holy Spirit to be your Mr. Miyagi?

Verse eleven - *Put on the whole armour of God that you may be able to stand against the schemes of the devil.* It is our responsibility to put on the whole, not partial, armour of God. Just like all the fruits of the spirit are connected together for us to walk in this life effectively, so is our armour. If one armour is missing, we are vulnerable. God wants us to be strong enough to withstand- withstanding means not to engage in, not to fall in, and not to entertain. That when you withstand a temptation that temptation has nothing to connect to in you. See, temptations are things that pull its comparison. A temptation is something that when something is brought into your presence, it's scanning you to see if there is anything in you that they can pull out of you that matches what is tempting you.

So, if you've got lust in you and a woman walks by, the woman and the lust in you will connect because the lust wants what it sees will satisfy it. If you see a bunch of money in front of you or an opportunity in front of you and you have greed, your greed will try to latch on to that opportunity. That's why you've got to make sure that you're strengthened in God and that you are led by the Lord's lordship so that nothing outside of you that's tempting or not for you won't pull it out of you. The goal is for all the temptations to no longer be temptations but to be test. Mature believers go through tests; weak believers fall into temptations. You can still be a strong believer and fall into temptation, but it shows that you were weak in that moment, but that mature believer will not stay in that temptation long. – The best way to avoid temptations is to never enter them.

Let's look at the definition of a scheme. A scheme is devious plan with the intent to do something illegal or wrong. The devil is a schemer his main objective including everyone connected to him is to find ways to destroy the key areas of your life. Satan's kingdom is legit and thriving and his goal is to develop a system so strong that if the days weren't shortened even Gods very elect would be deceived (Matthew 24:22). It is important to understand that Satan is not omnipresent like God. He wishes he could be everywhere and he is working hard to get to that place. His kingdom is full of demons and people whose objective is to advance the satanic cause which is to present the opposite of God in every arena. He has governments, resources, and high officials orchestrating his agenda. It's sad how many people are completely unaware of the schemes that are around them or that they are in. Right now, each of us are deceived about something, and it is due to a specific scheme tailored to us that may have been in our families for generations. Demons are strategic and specific they know more about your family then you do they know exactly how to implement a way of life into your life whether through friends, family tv or Netflix/ Hulu. Just about everything that is happening to you in the natural was sent specifically through the spiritual.

Nothing on this planet happens without a spiritual cause. Whatever effect is in your life right now was started by a spiritual cause. Every natural effect came from a spiritual cause. So many people think that these addictions came out of nowhere, these temptations came out of nowhere; no! These things were assigned, arranged for your downfall, and when you understand that, and you begin to respect your opponent, you will begin to decipher and discern before you engage in anything because you are now aware that schemes and plots are set against you.

When you go into the Federal Reserve they teach their employees not to study the fakes but to study the real, that when you study the real twenty-dollar, fifty dollars, or hundred-dollar bill over and over again then when the fake comes in your presence you will know the real so much, you will be able to spot the fake even if the fake look real, because you know the details, you know the ins and outs of the real. And when you begin to know God and engage with God and be around God, eat with God, pray to God, fast to God, sing to God, and house God in your heart then when you have anything demonic presented in front of you, even if it looks godly, even if it has a form of godliness you will know it doesn't have the power. That's why many believers have a form of godliness but denying the power thereof. I'd rather have the power than a form of it. We should all endeavour to be the real deal. This system has a huge bucket full of schemes set against you individually, corporately, financially, emotionally, and mentally. His schemes are set for your slip up. Walk carefully!

Verse twelve - *For we do not wrestle against flesh and blood but against the rulers, against the authorities, against the cosmic powers over this present darkness, against spiritual forces of evil in the heavenly places.* Let's break this down. Since the beginning of time we have been wrestling with the effects, but never the cause. Most, if not all, natural effects come from some spiritual cause. Satan wants us to wrestle with the natural and never unite to address the scheme and spiritual causes. If you wrestle against flesh and blood and only wrestle with what you see then you have been hoodwinked by what you can't see. If all you know is the natural, you will be easily deceived by the spiritual forces behind it. Every natural effect comes from a spiritual cause. When you understand that, anything that's presented to you naturally, you would not discern the natural effects, you would discern the spirit behind it. When a person always falls for what is at face value they will always fall on their face. But when you can discern deeper and see the face behind the value, then you will begin to say "This isn't valuable no more." Because when you discern the face behind the value you can say no to the value, because you now only want what God sends. When you know that you are wrestling against rulers, authorities, cosmic powers, and spiritual forces in the heavenly places, you will take your spirituality, your Christianity more seriously.

This verse also proves just how well-organized Satan's kingdom is. Satan has strongholds in every part of society and in most individual, he did this through rules and regulations. He did it through rulers meaning that there are people who try to rule over your life through influence, and their level of influence will begin to bring and spray suggestions into your life. He also does this by regulations. He knows for a fact if I can set rules against you, regulations in the spirit realm causing you to be depressed all the time, sad all the time, envious all the time, jealous all the time. Regulations set by the demonic kingdom to make sure you always envy somebody else's thing, or you are prideful in your own merit; then you will always fall. But when you know that God is stronger than all of these and he has given you authority over all of them, then you will walk and execute life differently.

Verse thirteen, *therefore take up the whole armour of God that you may be able to withstand in the evil day, and having done all, to stand firm.* You will not be able to be successful wearing partial armour; you've got to put on the whole armour of God. This verse gives you the glue; it gives you the focus of why everything needs to be worn. It says you've got to put on the whole armour of God. Why? That you may be able to withstand in the evil day. There is always going to be an evil day trying to make your blessed day evil. That's why when that evil day comes know on that day they are going to try and present a scheme, a plot a suggestion, and if you haven't been built up and have your whole armour on, then you won't be able to stand. Imagine a soldier in Afghanistan or the Gaza Strip, or wherever there is a war, and he or she doesn't have their helmet, gun, shoes or bulletproof vest he or she will be vulnerable. Even if they have nine out of the ten pieces of their armour, it only takes one bullet to hit them in the right place that's not guarded. You've got to ask yourself "Where in me am I vulnerable?"

Let's look at the armour - number one the belt of truth.

A belt represents the anchor point of the armour. Why do you think Paul inspired by the Spirit of God said 'the belt of truth'? Truth holds everything together, that when I have truth in an area, I'm tightened, I'm not loose. Imagine a soldier without a belt trying to run from an opponent or trying to run towards an opponent. Because of the things that are not tied in your life you have more of a chance of tripping than standing. When we don't have truth in an area, we become loose in that area. Truth tightens; lies loosens.

That's why it is our responsibility to find the truth of all significant matters, the truth about companionship, the truth about marriage, the truth about money; not the world's truth, God's truth. And you can't find God's truth without God's manual. That's why you've got to make sure your life is buckled at the waist with the belt of truth, that you're ready because you're tightened, you're smart, you're wise, you're discerning, you're watchful and prayerful. The Bible says watch and pray lest you fall into temptation, the people who fall in temptations are those who are too distracted to watch or pray.

The Breastplate

Why did Paul say, 'the breastplate of righteousness'? The breastplate guards the heart. A lot of people maybe even you reading this book now deep down in your heart you feel unworthy. If you feel this way, then you must know the importance of having on the breastplate of righteousness. A person who has on the breastplate of righteousness knows that they are saved not because of works but because of the gracious work of God. They know that they don't have to work for love just work from love. There is a difference. Those who are working for God's love do so because they feel unworthy those that are working from love work because they are worthy. God is not looking for perfection he is looking for progression anchored in the work of Jesus. It's hard to walk in love if you are not walking with Love. When we walk with God we will be renewed even during dark moments that we are loved and are capable of doing anything He has for us to do. I'm so glad he doesn't remember my sins. I'm so glad that when he sees me he sees Jesus' Righteousness that all I have to do is trust that as I walk with him, I will become new. Your righteousness cannot compare to the Righteousness of Jesus. Only those that are humbled understand this. So many people in the Church are trying to save themselves in their own righteousness. The bible says that our righteousness is as filthy rags. God doesn't care if our actions were right he cares if the motive behind the actions were. God is looking for a people that will do the right things for the right reasons because they are first submitted to him. We all do what's right for those we reverence and when you truly appreciate what Jesus has done for you; you can't help but do what's right. Now, will you do everything perfect no but you will at least have a heart that is in the right place with a motivation to it right the next time.

Our hearts must always be guarded by the Righteousness of Jesus if not we will continue to tangle ourselves in soul ties and strongholds. The beautiful thing about this is that He will cover those who desire to be covered. This reminds me of when Moses was with the children of Israel in Egypt. God commanded two of his servants to kill a lamb that was unblemished and to put the blood of the dead lamb on the doorpost of every person of Israel that when the death angel came and saw the blood on the door post it passed over it. It didn't matter if there was a homosexual in that room, it didn't matter if it was a liar in that room, it didn't matter if it was an adulterer in that room, it didn't matter if it was a whore in that room, the angel passed over because of the blood. People forget that just because I'm justified doesn't mean everything in me is out. When I'm justified in Christ, Christ has put the blood on my door post; the death angel has to continue to pass over. But I'm thankful that the same God that justified me by putting blood on my door post allows me to go through the Red Sea, and to allow myself to be purged crossing over from death to life and drowning all of my enemies in what was designed to drown me. That as I continue to grow, I might have been this person when I was justified, but through sanctification and his righteousness and his love, I'm a changed person. My heart needs that. It's nice nice to know that you don't have to work for his love. All you've got to do is walk in his love. My heart needs to know I don't have to work for forgiveness, all I've got to do is work from forgiveness.

With your feet fitted with the readiness that comes the gospel of peace.

This means that wherever I go I'm ready to bring the gospel and I am ready to bring peace. That doesn't mean I just go everywhere and just regurgitate the Gospel; it just means my life preaches the gospel! Many of us get so consumed in telling the gospel versus presenting the gospel through our life, showing people our scars and our wounds and how they were healed. When Jesus came to Thomas, Thomas didn't care about seeing Jesus; he wanted to see the wounds. You see, people will want to meet your saviour when you allow them to see your wounds, when you show them that you have scars they will see that someone healed you. Your scars are your stories they represent where injury once was, that when Thomas saw that the holes was in his hands and a hole was in his side, proof that he was saved, proof that he was redeemed the same Doubtful Thomas became

Dedicated Thomas. When you hide your wounds, they can't see where you were resurrected from.

But I also must have my feet fitted. There's nothing like shoes that can't fit. My shoes have to be tight, my gospel, my lifestyle has to be tight. I have to have peace tightened on my life that wherever I go my feet become the feet of Jesus bringing peace wherever I go. God's gospel and my feet have to become one. And they must be ready, and they have to be peaceful. God doesn't want you running up on people being loud, "Have you heard of the gospel?!" He doesn't want you running up on people; he just wants you to walk throughout life gently. And as people begin to see your walk with God, they will begin to say I want that kind of walk too. But your shoes must be tightened, fitted, ready. So, whenever God says "Go over there", you're ready to go. But you also got to make sure you have good shoes, because if you're out there with no shoes, then you're going to be hindered along the way. Good shoes keep you from nails. The Gospel keeps you from walking on things that will hurt you, because you know the truth.

Take up the shield of faith with which you can extinguish all the flaming darts of the evil one. Faith swallows flaming arrows. Satan doesn't care about who you follow; he just cares about your faith in the one you follow. he doesn't care that you follow Jesus or even if you are saved he just wants to make sure you don't operate in faith from the saving work of Christ. If he has your faith, he has your follow through. Faith helps you follow through, faith in God helps you to follow through on your purpose, follow through on your marriage, follow through on your manhood, follow through on your womanhood. If you don't have the shield of faith then you are always going to fall. That's why you've got to take up the shield of a faith with which you can extinguish the flaming darts. Your faith is what combats the flaming darts which are flaming suggestions, suggestions that are designed to gain root in your life.

Look at what Jesus was tempted by; he was tempted to turn stones into bread, meaning the devil was trying to tempt Jesus into fulfilling in his own hunger. But what Satan didn't realize was that Jesus hunger was the will of God. His faith was not in what he could do for himself but what the father already done for him. The enemy wants us to put the bulk of our faith in everything else but God and to provide for ourselves beyond the provisions of God. So many of us are in debt due to us trying to feed ourselves and not putting our faith in God.

He even tempted him to jump off a pinnacle. The purpose of Satan tempting Jesus to jump was to try to get Jesus to become famous before his time, to become known before his time. Jesus knew that a spectacular event wouldn't save anyone, because if that was so, the 5000 people that he fed the five loaves and three fishes to wouldn't have been asking for Barabbas later, because he knew just how fickle people were. He wants the people who are his remnant, who wants to follow him because of him. Jesus always chose the humble road because the humble road is always the best. Many of us are so desperate to be known that we would jump off of Everest just to get likes. Why try so hard to be known by man when God desires to know you…

He also tempted him to bow down and worship him; Satan said "If you bow down and worship me, I'll give you all the kingdoms." Why would Jesus bow down to Satan's kingdom when his kingdom trumps his kingdom? If he's the King of kings, then his kingdom is above all kingdoms. He had more faith in God's timing, more faith in God's provision, more faith in God's moment than he did doing it in his own efforts. So when the flaming darts are thrown at you, you have the faith to know that God will provide even if it seems like you're not being provided for. Faith is trusting in God and God's ability through you.

Notice the shield is not on the body but a tool that extends from the body. Your faith is beyond you shielding you from the vulnerable you. Having faith in God is supernatural because having faith in God goes beyond conventional wisdom. What's aimed at you should hit your faith before it hits your flesh. Meaning your faith should be such a thing that it exuded from you and before that dart can reach your mind or heart its quenched by your faith in God. Jesus was frail physically in the wilderness; he was hungry and tired but what the enemy tried to send his way was quenched in his faith in his Father.

Take the helmet of salvation.

A head shot is more lethal than a body wound. You've got to know why you're saved. The helmet covers the head; it covers the mind. I've got to know that I'm saved, I've got to know that I'm converted. Because I don't have to worry about condemnation when I fall, I don't have to worry about when I mess up because I know that God, if I confess my sins, he'll be faithful and just to forgive me of them all and turn my mess into a message. I saw a meme on Instagram that said that a prince or a princess is the only one that can wake up a king at 3 a.m. A king's child is the only person that can wake up a king at 3 a.m.; that's the same with our God. That if I'm adopted, and I'm accepted, then I have access. I've got to know that I'm justified, that I'm his son. When I know that I'm his son and I know that I'm saved I can walk confidently. It goes deeper I can't just know that I'm saved, I've got to see fruits that I'm saved. The Bible says I've got to walk out my salvation with fear and trembling (Phil 2:12), meaning that I've got to walk out my salvation with reverence and dependency. Trembling doesn't mean "Oh my I'm scared." It just says I've got to walk out my salvation knowing that I can't do it on my own merit, knowing that I need God, I need to see fruit to know that I'm saved. But when you see fruit - you're more loving than you used to be, you're more joyful in God than you used to be, you're more gentle and kind than you used to be, you're more long-suffering than you used to be, you have more self-control against sex and pornography and gluttony than you used to - then when anything comes at your mind against that you can fight it knowing that, you're saved by the blood of Jesus, and nothing they have to say can affect who you are. Because if I'm in God's hands, no one can pluck me out of that hand (John 10:28). There is a battle after what you know and how much you believe in what you know, and you just better make sure you have your helmet on.

It says, also take with you the sword of the spirit, which is the word of God. You've got to know your word; your word is your only weapon. The only weapon that Jesus used in the wilderness was the word. What you don't know in God's Word will be the angle that Satan comes against you. Satan comes at angles; he never comes straight at you. The demons come at angles; their angles are in the areas where you lack information, where you lack affirmation. They know for a fact that if you're not affirmed in what you believe, that's the angle they're going to attack you. If you're not informed about what you believe and informed about the word, that's the angle that they will attack you.

What area in your life lacks the word of God? Whatever place that is you've got to sharpen that area, you've got to know the word, you've got to sharpen that blade, you've got to know that thing in and out. You have to be familiar with your weapon. No good soldier is unfamiliar with their weapon. Their weapon is like an organ to them. Every word suggested to us by Satan we should only respond with the word of God so that when he tempts you about turning your stone into bread you'll know that God is your provider, when he tempts you to put yourself in tempting situations you will be able to say "I will not tempt the Lord my God." When he tempts you to bow down subtly or quickly, you'll know for a fact that you work for the kingdom of God whose kingdom is above any kingdom. If you don't have your blade sharpened and you don't work with that blade often, then when you are tempted you will fall. The worst thing is the imagery that I give most people, is that most people are held up when they are the officer, they are held up by a criminal with a snicker bar as a weapon. Imagine you go into a 7/11 or a Quick Trip, and you see a robber pointing a Snickers bar at an officer with a badge and a gun, expressing his authority and power and you see the officer with his hand up you will be confused because you're going to be like "What's a Snickers bar to a gun?" This happens to us all the time. We are being held up in our single lives, held up in our marriages and held up in our ministries and businesses by a criminal with no power.

As converted believers we have the badge which is our authority, which is the emblem that represents that we have the same authority as the one that enlisted us, and that we have the gun which is the word of God. When are you going to execute the authority God has given you? When are you going to execute the power that he's given you? It is important for you and me to put on all of these armours, because whichever one you do not have on your life, you won't be able to fight against the effects of a soul tie, the effects of a stronghold, or the demonic influences in our world today.

TRANSITION

For us to overcome our soul ties and our strongholds we need to know

- the core source,
- the core symptoms,
- and the core solutions.

Each one of us either struggle or have struggled with a soul tie or stronghold, and in order for us to overcome any of them we will need to know the the three items listed above. When we become familiar with these three things we will begin to have the right perspectives in overcoming our soul-ties. In the next few chapters I'm going to be discussing 9 different soul ties. In these chapters you will learn how to discover the core source of them, how to become aware of their symptoms and you will be equipped with resources to help you overcome them.

But you have to remember; you cannot overcome these things through natural means. Natural means may help you, it may be a means to help to an end, but it is not the main means to the end. What you need to know is how to break it spiritually, emotionally, mentally and physically. Each one of us, if you are a believer, have been set free; but it is our responsibility to walk in that freedom. The cage has been opened, the shackles have been broken, and all you've got to do is rise up and walk out. But the sad thing is many believers are still sitting in their cages with the doors open, and the shackles off. It would be crazy if you walked into a prison cell and the judge says this inmate you see in this cell has been set free for years but they are choosing for whatever reason not to walk in their freedom. Just like you would think that's crazy for that person to just sit there and not accept their freedom, you would be shocked to know that millions of "believers" who have been set free by Christ are still bound today. Are you one of them? Have you been set free but are allowing your insecurities, your emotional instabilities, your "mental illness" or your physical addictions to keep you from walking in your spiritual freedom?

If the spirit of God leads you, then your spirit will lead you to freedom. And the best way for the spirit to lead you to freedom is to lead you to the truth. The truth is in Christ; in Christ, you are set free.

He says, "Those that are in me are free and free indeed." You have been set free over 2,000 years ago, but you've been staying in the same prison cell for two years, 20 months, 20 years, two days… how long are you going to stay in that open cage? Today God wants to set you free.

In this book you will have prayers to pray over yourselves, you will have scriptures to memorize, and you will have different tools and resources to help you to walk in freedom in each of these areas whether it be all of these areas or just one. Each area will have its own plan to help you walk in that freedom.

Are you ready to walk through the cage door? If so lets continue →

CHAPTER THREE - ANGER

Why are you angry? What made you resentful? When you answer these questions, you will begin the process to setting yourself free from anger. The ultimate suggestions we hear from the enemy when it comes to anger is that we have the right to be angry, the right to be bitter, and the right to be upset. But what wrongs does that "right" fix? We can't always control what happens to us or even the feelings that arise within us, but we can control our actions. The enemy designed a system to have us impulsive and easily offended. He wants us overly attached to people, places and things that if anything happens to anything we care too much about we will be reactive instead of proactive. Now I understand that there is a fine line especially if something happens to a dear loved one, but we need to make sure that we build a firm and dependent spirit in God so that before, God forbids, severe moments come that we act biblically and not in full anger.

The Core Source
Anger is an emotion that is attached to a perspective. How I see what I see will to a degree determine how I feel about what I see. The most influential people in our world are those that under immense pressure can exercise self-control and self-discipline. God desires for us to have self-control and it's impossible to have this without self-discipline. A poor perspective and the lack of self-discipline are the core reasons why anger runs rampant. The enemy wants us to feel deeply not biblically he wants his system to determine how we feel. He wants us impulsive and always ready to defend. Before you defend anything, you have to depend and discern. Depend on God and allow his spirit to lead you into discerning every heighten situation. It's crazy how many of us stay in heighten situations instead of leaving them. A lot of people have lost their lives or have led to the loss of someone else's life due to them having to defend something. Nothing is worth defending in a dangerous situation that has an opportunity for you to escape it. Satan wants us overly dependent on our views and perspectives that at the moment those views, or valuables are threatened we defend impulsively without thinking. How do you respond when your emotions are heightened?

*There are situations where you will have to defend yourself immediately… the points above pertain to situations that you have an opportunity to avoid or leave.

When people are angry, they are usually angry because of what has happened to them, or what hasn't happened to them. They are trapped in a mind state that feeds their mind continuously about what they didn't deserve and what they do deserve.

When a person harbours these perspectives at high levels, they set themselves up to be easily triggered even if what triggered them doesn't apply to these extremes. Meaning when a person is harbouring intense feelings about a matter and haven't confessed or processed them, anything that crossed their path whether it be getting cut off in traffic or getting bumped into that innocent situation pokes at their bubble of anger and out of it comes rage. It's pointless to carry non-possessed anger because it only leads to more negativity.

Let's look at some core sources of enraged anger –
1. Un-forgiveness,
2. Resentment,
3. Bitterness,
4. The need for control,
5. Manipulation,

Let's look at un-forgiveness, resentment, and bitterness. Un-forgiveness, resentment, and bitterness are the murky residues of hurt. Hurt has a way of deepening emotional and mental wounds. A lot of our hurts either comes from us expecting humans to help our deepest needs or from our own hidden habits. Our need for help often hurts us the most. When you go to someone expecting them to help you more than God can, then that person will inevitably hurt you. Because when you put God like expectations on a human, that person will hurt or disappoint you. When you put all your eggs in a human's basket, those eggs will eventually crack.

But there's one soft place you can put all your eggs in, and that's in God. When you put your everything on him, he will never hurt you. The only way God will "hurt" or "disappoint" you is when you put false expectations on God and his will for your life. This is the only time God will disappoint you. God will not budge beyond his will and his timing for you. Your cooperation and your obedience according to his will and his timing will always lead to your protection and your promotion. It's crazy how many of us are mad at God because he doesn't answer our selfish prayers. God loves you too much to give you something he knows will separate you from Him and destroy you and everything connected to you. God just doesn't think about you he thinks about the safety and the maturity of everything connected to you. Before you pray, you must ask yourself "do I match what I am praying for?", if not then prepare for what you're praying for. Trusting God leads to safety and understanding. We must trust him even if we don't understand. We must trust him even during betrayal, abuse, a divorce or the loss of a loved one we must trust him because if not that rage will ruin what's left in our lives. He must be our sole help. No one else can help us like him. We must allow him to be the first responder to our emergencies we must make it our mission to seek Him first. Now I'm not saying people can't help us, but they can't be our first responders. Whoever you call on first will be the first responder. Let God be first and then let him show you who will be second if that person is needed.

When we put our ultimate trust in others over God, we will always be left disappointed. Our anger towards many of the people we are angry with today can be traced to a moment of trust. We trusted them to be a perfect help. No one can help you perfectly they can only help you based on their current level of self-awareness, wisdom, empathy, energy, and understanding. When a person is void of any of these traits they, if you put too much trust in them, will disappoint you. Some of us are mad at people and have no reason to be mad. We are mad because they haven't responded or have responded below our un-communicated expectations. It's one thing to put communicated expectations on a person and they don't meet them but it's another thing to put un-communicated expectations with the expectation of them meeting them. No one can read your mind but everyone to a degree can read your actions. Never expect from others what you are not expecting from yourself and never expect from others what God doesn't even expect from them. Meaning, don't expect a person to workout at a level you are not, or to eat healthy at a level you are not or to be something to you that you are not to them or even to yourself. And don't expect from them what God doesn't expect from them meaning don't expect for them to be yours if it's not in Gods will for them to be yours or to expect them to live in a city or fulfil a purpose God never intended for them to do or go. These uncommunicated expectations lead to embarrassment and worthless anger. God must be your everything so that he can instil in you the proper levels of empathy, understanding, and patience for everything else.

Satan's ultimate objective is for our hearts to be hardened whether through legit reasons or non-legit ones. And the best way for this to happen is for us to put our ultimate trust and hope into anyone else but God. He knows that when we do this, we will always end up disappointed. People can only help us to a certain limit. We are all limited. Satan wants us only to see a portion of what's presented and to have a false view on the potential of what's presented... meaning he wants us only to see a person's best and their potential. He knows that everyone always shows their BEST, first and within the span of a few months, while seeing their best and hearing their potential, we then put too much trust in them. So, while you are talking to this young man all you see and hear is his best and see his potential not knowing that lying in him are habits and hindrances that will soon hurt you. Be very careful what you accept into your life. Watch everyone's commercial all the way through. We all are aware of the pharmaceutical commercials that with their gentle music and wit say things like this product will help cure your back pain it will help you walk and talk again etc. but as you continue to listen under all of that music and great acting you also hear that this product may cause blindness, cancer or even death. Some of us don't discern people thoroughly, we harbour emotional needs and allow those needs to lure us into the arms or into situations whose side effects are worse than the pain we are currently going through. It is best to trust God and push these individuals to the side than to push God away and suffer the consequences of their side effects. Now no one is perfect but the people God places in your life their flaws will not be worse than what you are currently going through. Satan loves the effects of side effects in our lives. He loves when we bring ticking time bombs into our lives. Bombs that have a set time to them where they end up cheating, mistreating and abusing you. Their time of being fake is up, and their true color's begin to show but it's too late for you because you have invested your mind, body, soul and time into them and now you are left with a bitterness that over time turns into resentment and un-forgiveness. When you put any substantial amount of trust into anyone you will be left bruised. When a human is bruised and doesn't go to God first they will continue to deepen that bruise. God is the only physician able to heal the soul. I always tell people if you were hurt in the game called love before you enter back in let Dr. Love heal you and rehab you. So many of us get hurt and then jump right back onto the field without giving ourselves time to heal and that bruise gets worse and worse.

Now that bruise turns into a mind state of bitterness meaning you just have this pool of negative emotions swimming in you and as bitterness settles and forms your perspective on that individual hardens into resentment. Once resentment settles you begin to blame everything on them or that situation, and now you have anger in your mind that is "valid" that even at the mentioning of their name your face tightens and your heart races. Once you adopt the demonic idea that this person or persons are the sole blame for your demise, you begin to harbour unforgiveness. Un-forgiveness is Satan's number one tool that keeps people from checking their part and God's part in the narrative. No matter what you are going through or have gone through understating your sins towards a Holy God will help you process through the sins that have happened to you. When you consult God and are honest with Him about your feelings you will begin to have the same sentiments that Jesus did on the Cross when he said father forgive them for they know not what they are doing and then over time you will begin to see the fruit of that hurt noticing that if they didn't betray you, abuse you or hurt you-you wouldn't be the person you are today.

Sometimes promotions require a Judas. Some of the people that played a part in hurting us didn't know what they were doing and even If they did know, know that God uses all scraps to help develop our lives. See beyond what happened to you and see what could happen if you simply forgive. Forgiveness may not change them but it will certainly change you. Now don't get me wrong forgiveness doesn't always mean the rekindling of friendships; you don't have to be friends with them it just means that you're letting go in your heart the offences they have caused in your life and seeing them how Christ sees them and trusting that these scraps will be used soon for your favour.

Forgiveness works for you; un-forgiveness works against you. Who is that person you need to forgive? Whoever that person is, forgive them quickly. It's crazy how we are slow to forgive but expect God to forgive us quickly. Don't you know we are all guilty of murder? The sins that required the death of Jesus over 2000 years ago wasn't just the sins of His day but all of our sins. My sins and your sins and everyone's sins played a huge role in murdering Jesus. We may not have been the one to beat him, nail him or pierce him but we all played a role for the NEED of his death. All sins from every sinner was laid on him and this person Jesus looks at us every day and despite our role opens his arms to forgive us. I'm so thankful that he was disciplined and understanding enough to see beyond my sins to see who I could be in him and love me for it. I'm so glad that Jesus didn't harbour any bitterness or resentment towards me because if He did, he would have left me with me and with a dying world. You in your own effort will not be able to comprehend or be consistent with forgiveness it is only in the renewing of your minds through the spirit of God that you can. He alone the supreme master of forgiveness can teach us how to forgive. Forgiveness releases the effects of anger. Forgive quickly as God ever so quickly forgives us.

Who are the people that have deeply hurt you?	What did they do to hurt you?	What part may have you played?	How could God use this hurt to help mature you?

Let's talk about the need for control and manipulation.

Some people use fake anger as a tool to control and to manipulate others into bending to their carnal needs. Listen, if you're around somebody who's always angry and they try to make you feel bad for what you may have done to them, you've got to let that person go or you've got to love them from afar. Because that person will continue to use their anger against you for their good. You've got to be able to embrace self-respect. It doesn't matter who the person is, or what you may have done you are no one's doormat. You must forgive yourself and respect yourself and let that person know you will not be affected by their anger. Now if it's a person that is trying but what you may have done to them really affected them in a bad way then you need to be gracious and understanding, but if things are going beyond your place of self-respect then they will need to heal alone. A lot of people are up under manipulation due to guilt and or the desire to be accepted. Satan's goal with this is to utilize other peoples anger to control the progression of others.

Manipulative people desire to mould others into pawns. Many of these people are unaware that they are the host of a Jezebel spirit. The Jezebel spirit is a spirit of control. This spirit is no respecter of gender seeing that men host this spirit as well. This spirit seeks insecure, bitter and vindictive people to manipulate other weak and misguided individuals. This spirit will take any opportunity to control other people lives, businesses, ministries, families etc. It will use your jealousy, anger, and envy as a tool to hurt others. Hurt people hurt people and hurt people are the perfect host for the spirit of Jezebel.

Let's talk about being easily offended. A person who is continuously angry is a person who is easily offended. I have a saying that I say all the time 'offense hinders offence', meaning a person who is easily offended is never on the offense, they are always on the defence. They are always defensive; they are never offensive. Offense means scoring, means advancement, means winning. You cannot win if you don't put any points on the board. If you're always defending and never scoring, you'll never win. When people are easily offended they hinder their offense, and sometimes the offense of others. When a team is upset with each other, it hinders their court play. The same is with us when we are easily offended; any and everything will be used to hinder our progression. We've got to make sure we're not allowing anything to be used to hinder us from progressing.

Making assumptions.

I always tell people 'ask before you assume.' People who are easily offended always make assumptions; they're too insecure to ask. They rather hold on to an assumption, so they can feel empowered, emboldened even, so they can stay upset with you. But if you want true freedom, you will never let anything rest at assumption. If you want closure; ask for it. If you want to know what really happened; ask. Many people have allowed themselves to be alienated due to assumptions. Before you assume anything about a person, ask that person. If you have the courage to assume about a person have the courage to ask that person because if you ask you will at least have the opportunity to have the truth. If you assume then you will be imprisoned by the 'what if'.

Have you ever been in a place where assumptions led to your destruction? That you assumed and your assumptions broke up your marriage, your assumptions broke up your part in the church; your assumptions broke up your business? That all of that could have been fixed and intact now if you would have just simply asked. Do not allow anger to build through assumptions, let anger be cancelled out by just simply asking. And if you ask that person and you don't get the answer that you thought you were going to receive, so what? At the end of the day, you have God. I tell people I would rather have God and lose everything than to have everything and not have God. Because if I have God and I lose everything, I ❀STILL ❀HAVE ❀EVERYTHING! Never give people too much power over you. Seek closure for yourself and if you don't receive anything let their silence be your closure.

Here are the core symptoms of a person who is angry –
1. Anger and resentment towards God,
2. temper problems
3. deep hatred
4. Self-hate
5. cursing,
6. seeking vengeance
7. violence,
8. physically and verbally abusive,
9. looking to retaliate,
10. envy and jealousy
11. judgmental,
12. always critical,
13. taking offense easily,
14. angry towards others,
15. unforgiveness
16. irritable,
17. angry towards authority,
18. manipulation,
19. racism

If any of these things are evident in your life, then you have a problem with anger. These symptoms if left undealt with will have you furiously tied to people and situations. They will birth strongholds in your life keeping you from forgiving and being free.

Core Solutions

Let's talk about some core solutions. Let's look at Ephesians 4:26-27. The Bible says, *be angry, and do not sin; do not let the sun go down on your anger and give no opportunity to the devil.* According to this scripture, it's okay to be angry, but it's not okay to sin from anger. God is a realist; he knows that you're human, he knows you have emotions. The thing is, he wants you to have emotions, but not for your emotions to have you. When a person always allows their emotions to get the best of them, they always find themselves in situations where they have to apologize, to forgive, to try to rekindle or to try to build back that bridge that they've burnt. It's okay to be upset but you've got to know how to process that anger, because if you're always offensive and you're always offended, then it shows you have no processes or systems in your life to handle that anger. You've got to make sure you have things in place to help you process your anger. Do you have a cooldown corner? Do you have a cooldown place? Do you speak in tongues? Can you go to the bathroom and pray? What system do you have in place to nullify that anger? Because the longer you let that anger sit in, the more of a chance you will sin from it.

Never give full vent to your spirit, meaning never allow your spirit to release everything quickly. Never allow yourself to give over into anger. Anger and frustration is some of Satan's choice emotions to use because the bulk of people regret their actions once those emotions have settled. When a person sins from anger, they usually regret what they've done. God has a set time for anger –the set time is before the sun sets. Satan's goal is for anger to carry over into as many days as possible. The quicker a matter is settled, the less consequences can occur. The Bible says do not let the sun go down on your anger, meaning don't let any day go by without dealing with the anger of that day or the anger of the days before. The more days that carry over, the more opportunities we give the devil to work. You are more susceptible to acting according to the ways of Satan when you're angry. The fruit of Satan's kingdom comes from anger; he is angry at God and he is jealous of you. If you give Satan an inch, he will become a ruler, if you give him a little anger he will take it as far as you let him. What opportunities are you giving Satan? We are told that we wrestle not against flesh and blood but unseen entities behind them. The moment you wrestle with anger towards another person is the moment you lose.

Now the question is, how do I be angry and sin not?

1. Number one, you've got to establish a culture of peace and quick forgiveness. You do this by constantly reminding yourself of God's love and forgiveness towards you, as well as reminding yourself about the benefits of maintaining joy and peace. Never let anyone or anything steal your peace. Peace is priceless. Create a culture in your life where you maintain your peace.
2. Number two, give yourself time to process the consequences. Always process what could happen. I always tell people, think three moves ahead of every situation. Think yourself into trouble so that you won't end up in trouble.
3. Number three, remove yourself. It is better to leave a bad situation than to contribute to a bad situation. If you know it's bad; remove yourself. I rather take an L and keep my integrity and dignity than to stay and look like a fool. There is a saying from afar two people arguing both look like fools.
4. Number four, Establish support systems. Support systems are systems that ensure that you're held up in moments of testing or when pursuing goals. Seek counsel, have an emergency prayer spot, do deep breathing, meditate on God's word do whatever it takes to stay supported. Do you have things in place that will hold you up when you're angry?
5. Number five, remember they are human and this too shall pass. Listen, people are flawed; they're going to make mistakes, they're going to hurt you; move on.
6. Finally, look at every situation through the eyes of God. Could God be using this person to sharpen you? Could God be using this situation to test you, to test your long-suffering, to test your patience?

Let's look at James, James 1:19-20, *Know this my beloved brothers, let every person be quick to hear, slow to speak, slow to anger; for the anger of man does not produce the righteousness of God.* There's a difference between righteous anger and rotten anger. The difference between a righteous anger and a rotten anger is in the core - righteous anger stems from a righteous place and leads to a righteous outcome, while the rotten anger stems from a rotten place and leads to a rotten outcome. Rotten anger does not produce the righteousness of God. Righteous anger says I'm angry at what sin is doing in this person's life; I'm angry in what sin is doing in society, I'm angry at what sin is doing in me. Therefore, I have a righteous anger against the sin but not the sinner. I don't have a righteous anger towards myself or towards other people. Rotten anger is an anger that is infused with negative perspectives and aims to destroy everything against its agenda. Non-default human anger is a demon. Demons names are what they manifest through people. When we always allow ourselves to be angry our anger will attract the demonic spirit of anger and that demon then will lodge itself in you causing you not to receive or produce the righteousness of God.

Our objective should be always to produce a righteous outcome, and we do that by always being quick to hear, slow to speak, and slow to anger,' and we can't do this without God's self-control. Listen, self-control is one of the fruits of spirit; you can't be loving without self-control, you can't be patient without self-control. Self-control will keep you from going beyond restrictions. Let's break these three points down

'Quick to hear' - quick to hear means to be quick to understand and to be selfless as much as possible. In every conversation, we need to be quick to hear the other side with the intent of answering gently and intently. God wants us to hear before we speak; he gave us two ears and one mouth for a reason. 'Slow to speak' means to gather your answer before spewing your answer. Many people have said things they didn't mean while angry and they now regret them. Sometimes strongholds in others are built through words that were never meant to be spoken. Some people are bound because of what somebody else said, and that person didn't even mean what they said. Be very careful what you say and be very careful in entertaining what other people may have said about you. Does what they say about you match what God says about you? And does what you say about a person match what God says about them? If you don't watch your words, your words could be the stronghold in your daughter's life, in your husband's life, your wife's life, your son's life and in your congregant's lives.

'Hollow but heavy' - your words may be hollow to you but heavy to someone else. Words can be forgiven, but they can't be forgotten. Hollow words are words that was said while you were angry, but you didn't mean. Just because you didn't mean it doesn't mean it is not going to be heavy on the other person. The Scripture also says be slow to anger. Being angry is like carelessly burning fuel on something pointless. We must learn how to re-channel our anger to produce righteous outcomes. The best way to avoid anger is to be quick to hear, slow to speak and slow to anger.

Proverbs 29:11, A *fool gives full vent to his spirit, but a wise person quietly holds it back*. Never give full vent to your spirit, meaning never allow your spirit to release everything quickly. Never allow your heart to vent out all of its content without the proper processes. You've got to be able to process everything. Giving full vent to your spirit is like giving a drunk person a microphone. Don't give your heart a microphone when it's hurt. A wise person quietly holds it back knowing that winning the war is better than winning every battle. You can't win every battle, but through the right strategy you can win the war and winning the war could be winning your family member, co-worker or son back to Christ. Listen, sometimes it's best to be the bigger person and lose the battle and let that person think they've won but you know deep down that you did the right thing.

Proverbs 19:11, *Good sense makes one slow to anger, and it is the glory to overlook an offense*. It makes good sense to overlook an offense and to be slow to anger. It makes sense because you 1) won't say something you will regret, 2) you know you ultimately don't wrestle against flesh and blood, 3) you will have a better chance of winning that person over through kindness than through anger, 4) you won't look stupid in public nor waste your time, and 5) you know that a soft answer can turn away anger. It takes wisdom to drain away tension.
Proverbs 15:1 is another good scripture. *A soft answer turns away wrath, but a harsh word stirs up anger*. Tone is a key part of communication. How you say what you say matters. Words filled with anger can really penetrate to the vulnerable parts of a person. When someone is angry, it's better to respond gently than harshly. Your soft answer of understanding can really calm a person down. We don't always know the triggers of others and sometimes what we say can really affect them. Each and every one of us have struggles, and each of us have areas that we sometimes value to the extreme and when those areas are touched with harsh or joking words those words can cause a harsh non joking reaction. Empathy and understanding can really calm the energy of anger in a person. It's better to turn away wrath for the safety of everyone than to stir it up and cause more problems.

Now let's talk about how to untie a root of anger:

Number one, you've got to learn how to forgive. You've got to forgive yourself and forgive others. You've got to go to the core of that anger and ask why am I so angry? Who am I mad at and what am I mad at and why. Answering the why will help you with who or what you are mad at. What is the anger connecting you to and what is this anger keeping you from? Are you still upset years after what made you upset? How many days have you allowed to past with anger still in your heart? It's crazy how many people can't enjoy their husband or wife because they are still upset with their ex. It's crazy how many people can't enjoy the season they are in or enter a new season God has for them because they are still angry. You've got to let those things go or those things will keep you from progressing. The best way to overcome a present or past situation is to ask yourself, "What is this present thing or present person or negative situation keeping me from?" You've got to teach yourself how to cool down, you've got to set systems and processes in place, and you've got to forgive yourself. My question to you is, are you ready to break this area? If so go through the checklist and repeat the prayer below.

Anger						
How strong is the tie or hold in this area? →				Weak	Mild	Strong
Which areas are affected and in what way? Place a check beside each area that's affected and explain in what way in the larger box below.						
Spiritually		Mentally		Emotionally		Physically

Father in heaven,
I am thankful that you are not angry towards me. I am thankful that you have forgiven me that you love me beyond my own ability to love myself and I am thankful for your expression of Love through Jesus. Father, I repent for being angry at me, at others, at past situations, and even mad at you. Right now, Heavenly Father, cleanse me from all anger, untie my heart from anything that I am angry about. Lord I forgive myself, I forgive the following individuals

_____

_____

_____ ,

and I repent for harbouring resentment for the following situations

_____

_____

_____

Heavenly Father, give me the right perspective on these things. Help me to see this situation, these individual how you see them.

Right now through the authority of Jesus Christ I come against every demonic spirit of anger, resentment, manipulation, against every Jezebel spirit, I come against every scheme of the enemy that's causing me to lose from being angry. I've repented, and I've confessed. Therefore, I have the authority against you right now Satan. You will no longer have a place through anger in my heart. I command you to lose me here now and forever. I break this soul tie and stronghold in the spirit realm, and I will be untied and loose from this day going forward in my emotions, mind and body. I will walk out of this cage free from anger right now in Jesus Name.

Father, I turn my attention back to you, thank you for setting me free. I will now set up support systems that I need to stay free. I thank you Father, and I love you, in Jesus' name I pray. Amen.

Now that you have broken it in the spirit-realm lets develop systems and process to help you break it in the natural.

70x7 Plan

First, I want you to list again everyone who has hurt you to the point that you may still feel a certain way about them. You have forgiven them, but your emotions and mind still need some more time to heal. Next to their names I want you to write down the thoughts and the feelings you feel every time they are mentioned or every time they cross your mind. Once you have done this I want you to write down some positive things about that person and ways you can pray for them. The bible says in Matthew 5:43-48

43 "You have heard that it was said, 'You shall love your neighbour and hate your enemy.' 44 But I say to you, love your enemies and pray for those who persecute you, 45 so that you may be sons of your Father who is in heaven. For he makes his sun rise on the evil and on the good and sends rain on the just and on the unjust. 46 For if you love those who love you, what reward do you have? Do not even the tax collectors do the same? 47 And if you greet only your brothers, what more are you doing than others? Do not even the Gentiles do the same? 48 You therefore must be perfect, as your heavenly Father is perfect.

Once you have finished this exercise I want you to every time you think about them to think on their positives and ways to pray for them. Praying for others has a way of building empathy and it is through empathy that we can defuse anger. Jesus was asked by Peter in Matthew 18:21-22

21 "Lord, how often will my brother sin against me, and I forgive him? As many as seven times?" 22 Jesus said to him, "I do not say to you seven times, but seventy-seven times.

Jesus is letting us know that it doesn't matter what the law says about only forgiving a person a handful of times he says every time you see or think about them forgive them. You may not see them 70x7 times but you sure will mentally and every time they come up mentally we are commanded to forgive and that goes for your sins against yourself. You must let go of your anger towards you. Work through the exercises below and walk in your freedom.

Persons or Situations Name →		
Thoughts	Feelings	Positives and Prayers

Persons or Situations Name →		
Thoughts	Feelings	Positives and Prayers

Persons or Situations Name →		
Thoughts	Feelings	Positives and Prayers

Persons Name →		
Thoughts	Feelings	Positives and Prayers

Persons Name →		
Thoughts	Feelings	Positives and Prayers

Cool Down Techniques

Physically being in a hot area for a long period of time can lead to heat exhaustion, dehydration or heat stroke. The same is with our emotions. The longer you allow your inner self to sit in the hot conditions of anger, resentment and unforgiveness you will suffer drastically. To avoid these heat or anger related symptoms you must learn how to cool down. Take some time below to develop your cool down techniques. Write down your causes or triggers and write down how you plan to cool down when heated.

What causes you to get heated at times? – Triggers	What can you do or where can you go to cool down when heated in these areas?
1.	
2.	
3.	
4.	

CHAPTER FOUR – FEAR AND PROCRASTINATION

Fear, by definition or if I can give it an acronym, is F.E.A.R "False Evidence Appearing Real." Anytime you experience fear, you are encountering a false evidence. Even though the situation appears real or feels real, it doesn't mean that it is. In life, you either walk by faith or by fear. Unfortunately, many people have allowed the false evidence that comes before them because of its authentic appearance and feeling to keep them from walking in the promises of God. Many people have forsaken their opportunities to walk by faith because they have allowed fear to paralyze them. You see, demons love to exude an aura of fear from their presence that causes you to believe what you feel is more real than what is on the opposite side of what you're facing. Fear will always try to keep you from going beyond every wall that God has called you to climb over.

But imagine who you could be and what you could accomplish if you go beyond that barrier of fear. Never let a false evidence become real! It is so sad that the truth seems fake. It seems that the things we're supposed to do feel like they're not true but the things that we should avoid are real; that's the way fear cripples us. It keeps us from flourishing and going forward. God wants you to be stretched into a place called "the uncomfortable." However, fear keeps you from uncomfortable places. Unlike what you may believe, it is the uncomfortable place that strengthens and stretches you. It is in the position of discomfort where you discover what you were created to be. No wonder the Devil loves it when you remain in complacent zones, rather than creative zones. Because when you're creative, you will always press forward. But when you allow fear to grip you, it will paralyze and keep you from flourishing. Anything that keeps you from flourishing prevents you from bearing fruit. And the worst thing for the Devil is a person who bears good fruits.

Fear keeps us from progressing. A lot of people allow the fear of failure to keep them from moving forward. Such fear becomes a stronghold, a mental crutch, and a mental barrier. Many people don't even try because they believe they will fail. But like I tell everyone, failure teaches you how to succeed; it lets you know if the plan needs to be changed completely or simply modified. It refines your purpose and destiny.

Insecurities and inadequacies cause us to be inactive and immobile. When a person feels insecure that person has an area that is not founded, that is not solid, that's not secured. When a person is secure and confident, nothing can push them away from accomplishing what they want to accomplish. When a person feels inadequate, they feel like 'I'm surrounded by smarter people, taller people, brighter people, and since I don't have this degree, since I don't have these accomplishments, since I don't have these accolades I shouldn't even try.' It doesn't matter what you don't have; it is about what you have on the inside. Because God doesn't care about qualifying the qualified. He qualifies the people whom he calls.

Never let your insecurities or inadequacies cause you to be inactive or immobile. The best way to keep a demonic kingdom progressing is to cause God's people to be inactive and immobile. Inactive meaning that you are not actively pursuing what you were created for. The worst thing that you could do is to pursue something you weren't created for. The best thing you could do is to go with all your might to be active in th e area you were created for. In order to do so you must first love him with all your heart. The weight of your heart determines your might. The lighter it is, the more you can do but the heavier it is, the less you can do. Satan also wants you to be immobile, stuck, not moving. He wants you to be in park. God has created you to drive, to go forward. Look at your face, everything on your face is forward - your eyes are forward, your nose is forward, your mouth is forward, even though your ears are on the side they're aimed like antennas forward. God created us to move forward. The sad thing is a lot of people are going forward just in the wrong direction.

What is that thing in your life that's causing you not to move forward? What are you really afraid of? What are you allowing to keep you from going in the direction you are supposed to? The one place you should be afraid of going towards is the place that you weren't created for because we all are going to be judged for the work we have done in this life.

What is procrastination:

Procrastination is pushing back what needs attention now. The best way to keep you from being free indeed is to have you push back the very things that will set you free. It's crazy how quickly we push back God and the things of God. We pull towards ourselves the things of the world and push away the things that have eternal value. God created systems of freedom which all start with Jesus. Jesus in any accepted area guarantees freedom. Where there is Jesus there is freedom where there is no acceptance of Jesus there is no freedom. Satan wants the name of Jesus to be unacceptable in as many places as possible. Isn't it strange that the most attacked name of all names is Jesus? All other names and titles are accepted but Jesus; I wonder why? Could it be that it is the most powerful name? Usually, the most hated name has the most power. Jesus' name carries weight but not too many people are ready to carry that name. The enemy hates where there is grace because where there is grace, there is power where there is grace there is Godly support. He doesn't really care if you know the name he just cares if you operate in the name. Operating in the name means operating in his assignment for you. Satan makes you powerless when he tempts you to forfeit your assignment in Christ. He knows that it is what's in your hands that will lead to other freedoms. Look at Moses and David each had something in their hands that led to freedom. When Moses asked God at the red seas what he needs to do God told Moses to use what's in his hands. When David was asked to use Saul's armour, he denied the request and used what was familiar in his hands. Moses used what was in his hands and parted the red seas David used what was in his hands to defeat Goliath both utilizing those items endowed with the power of God to provided freedom. Could it be that you are still stuck at the red sea still being taunted by giants all because you are not putting to work what's in your hands? Satan loves it when you swap with him. What he did to Adam and Eve he is still doing with us having us take out of our hands what will provide us freedom and putting in our hands what will keep us bound. God only goes half way. He only went the whole way once, and that was to the cross he now says to us that we now have something that those in the previous covenant didn't have and that's power. We don't have to wait for the spirit of God to come upon us we now have him in our hearts.

It all boils down to energy. The enemy will add into your life things that will drain you of your energy affecting your execution. Less is more and more is less. The less you have the more you can get done the more you have the less you will get done. Based on your current life habits (sleep, eating, etc.) you produce a certain amount of energy. There are a few stages of energy

1. A lot of energy
2. Some energy
3. A little energy
4. No energy
5. Burn out

Your lifestyle habits matter to God. He cares about how much you sleep get; He cares about what you eat and how you manage your energy, because He can only use what's in you. Don't give God what's left over give God your first. When you continuously aim to give God, you, he will infuse in you, supernatural energy but he will not give energy to a person that is executing in sin. You will be left with your own energy. People want God to use them in a mighty way but don't know how to manage their own energy. You must manage your energy. You must manage your spiritual, emotional and mental energies keeping leaches away. Satan wants you at stage burn out. He doesn't want you with a lot of energy. The greatest energy on the planet for the believer is Joy. And the best way to steal your joy is to lure you away from the presence of God. Sin separates. It separates you from God, from your loved ones, from grace, from love, from peace it separates you from your power source. Satan wants you to be in debt with your energy. Every time you sin significantly you are transferring your energy to the demons assigned to you. They feed off your actions. Your actions solidify them having a place to stay. Sin feeds them; accepted sanctification starves them. When you allow the work of God in your life and you through repentance press after him, you will be empowered. The safest place on earth is in the presence of God; it is safer to be in a wild jungle where God is than in a mansion full of security without him. Which kingdom is thriving off your energy? Which kingdom are you producing for? What are you allowing to distract you from being productive for God? Every day for the next week you should calculate where your natural energy goes and monitor what receive the most attention. Really look and see where the bulk of your energy is going. All of us produce, but not too many of us if we are honest are producing for the development of our spirits. Our flesh is obese, and our spirits are anorexic.

30-day energy tracker
List beside each number under activity, what you do on a normal day/week and beside that the time you typically spend with it. Utilize the 7-day tracker below to get a glimpse of where your energy flows by placing beside the activity the time you spent with that person or thing that day.

Activity	Time
1	
2	
3	
4	
5	
6	
7	
8	
9	
10	

Days	Day 1	Day 2	Day 3	Day 4	Day 5	Day 6	Day 7
Activity 1							
Activity 2							
Activity 3							
Activity 4							
Activity 5							
Activity 6							
Activity 7							
Activity 8							
Activity 9							
Activity 10							

Reflection:

Constant fellowship with God is the answer to us overcoming our fears. Whatever you fellowship with the most you will have faith in the most. Whoever you allow to teach you most you will trust most. Satan hates a talented, creative person that refuses to leave God's presence. Satan hates a person that uses worship power instead of willpower to avoid sin he hates it because he knows with you and Gods power and abilities combined you will usher a move of God in your area of influence. Every believer when they spend time with God receives a new log on their fire. Their spirit becomes recharged and any fire whether little or small applied to the right kind of surface will spark a fire. He hates it when we are on fire because we can be used to burn up his plans in the lives of others. Fire = enlightenment. Not the evil light of the new age but the original light of the renewed age. We must never forget that a fire with no logs dies.

Times are too evil for us to be distracted. God wants us to be disciplined and discerning not dumb and distracted. When we are distracted destruction increases but when we are disciplined and discerning destruction decreases. Now don't get me wrong God doesn't want us to live a boring mundane life He promised us an adventurous and amazing life full of joy. He just wants to make sure his people are putting things in their rightful place. The definition of a distraction is anything that is engaged with before something more important. There is nothing wrong with extracurricular activities, but when they come before family, God or your health it's a distraction. Imagine how many things have been destroyed due to seasons of you being briefly distracted? How much did your relationships, your projects, your health suffer all due to a brief moment of enjoyment? Distractions can be deadly.

Fight fear with Faith.

Faith is the substance of things hoped for, the evidence of things not seen, meaning faith is more tangible than you know. Everybody walks by faith every day to some degree. If you're sitting in a chair right now you're walking or sitting by faith right now. Your faith in the chair you are sitting in is due to the chairs faithfulness. Since the chair has proven to you to be faithful you don't think twice to put your faith in it. But the moment that chair proves to be unfaithful you will stop putting your faith in it. Our faith is predicated on our perspectives. The people with the right perspectives on God, their life and the items around them will be able to feel the substance of their faith and see the evidence beyond what they see. But when you are a prisoner of sight, you lose the ability to discern deeper. So many people are soul tied to past moments, soul tied to the wrong people due to them not seeing beyond what they see. Faith in God requires us to see what he sees and to see it correctly.

The Bible says that faith comes by hearing and hearing by the word of God meaning that our sight becomes refined when we continuously hear the word of God. Now, this hearing doesn't mean the voice of a preacher, but it means the voice of God. Reading the Bible without the Holy Spirit is a waste of time. Memorizing scripture without meditating on it is pointless we must seek the word of God so that we will be conditioned to see how he sees. So many people have good sight but are walking blind; still attached to things that clearly through the eyes of God are wrong. We have all been there especially in relationships. It's hard to see what you're in when you are in it, but you sure see everything clearly when you take a few steps away from it. Infatuation and insecurities have a good way of blinding us from what is blatantly in front of us. That is why we must fellowship with God often because the level of our fellowship with Him will determine our faithfulness to him and to his principles. If you barely fellowship with him, you will barely walk in faith with him, if you periodically fellowship with him you will periodically walk in faith with Him, but if you always fellowship with him you will walk in faith at a high level. No fellowship no faith. More fellowship more faith. In life you are going to feel fear but fear cannot thrive in an intense fellowship with God.

Whatever you do mostly, you are walking by faith in that area. Many of us are grateful for our distractions and our "limitations" because they give us an excuse not to go hard after what God wants us to do. We love the phrase "well at least I tried" God never said that a trier of the word will be successful he said a doer of the word will. Just "trying" is proof that your faith is contaminated. If God tells you to do it, then he will fully equip you to do it. Take try out of your vocabulary and add the word do! As I have said, many times you are not going to be judged on what you tried to do but on what you did. Attempts do not matter to God; done does!

Walking with God and walking in faith is not easy or comfortable. God will always take you through places that will stretch you and the last time I checked stretching is not comfortable. Procrastination and fear loves comfort. They thrive in it. We love our comforts. Some of us love our couches more than we do going to the gym or our beds more than hard work. We love being comfortable. Fear gives us the excuse to choose comfort over conflict, challenges and over doing what it takes to be a champion in life. But it is our conflicts and challenges that develops our character. I'm sure you heard me say this on YouTube that we don't grow in comfort zone but in challenge zones. If what you are facing or doing is not challenging you then you are not growing. You need to have daily, weekly, monthly, quarterly and yearly challenges and systems to measure your growth. We should be growing every day because we will always have room to improve. Sanctification means becoming newer. The more you submit to the sanctification process of Jesus the more you will grow. When was the last time you grew? What do you have in place to challenge you?

Fear will have you surrounding yourself with comfortable friends, comfortable habits and comfortable entertainments and eliminate everyone and everything that challenges you. If you are comfortable you are complacent. Are you really at this point proud of you? Where in your life right now must you improve and what is keeping you from making those improvements? Forget the critics forget the discomforts you may feel with those that may not agree with you pursuing your new you. They don't want you to grow because your growth makes them uncomfortable. Walking by faith makes those who walk by fear very uncomfortable because your work ethic exposes their lack of commitment. Walking by faith is a long walk because not too many people are on that path. This faith walk is your faith walk and you must grow because those who need you need for you to be someday at your best. Your best life is a life of growth. Your best life is a life of faith in God but if you listen to everyone else's negative or positive unbiblical opinions then you will die and face God with the harsh reality that you didn't even live. Give yourself, life!

Moments

Tragic moments, transitional moments, theorized moments and testing moments have ways of birthing fear. The sin is not in feeling fear but acting in it. Satan wants us to operate unbiblically during these moments hoping to build a stronghold. He loves when we experience tragedy in an area because he knows that we will less likely walk in faith in that area.

He loves to torment us in moments of vulnerability or while transitioning. We are our most vulnerable when going through a transition. He loves to torment us when we are rising or falling. Transitional moments are where he uses the lack of resources against us. Transitional periods are dangerous for us because we are leaving what we are used to and are transitioning into a place we are not fully familiar with. We are leaving a place where we know every corner to a place where we are not quite comfortable. No matter which direction we go whether up or down transitions can be vulnerable. No matter where you go you have to always guard your heart against fear. If God is transitioning you, there is no need to fear.

Theorized Moments
We are vulnerable at times during our quest for knowledge. Many people lack self-discipline when it comes to educating themselves. People rather be fed knowledge than to hunt for it. Fear is birth in our hearts when what we know is threatened. The beautiful thing about life is that behind everything is a trail of truth! You can find the truth about anything if you search hard enough. God made sure belief in him can be proven. Why would God have a trail of lies leading to him? But most truth is hidden in plain sight, but most people are just too spiritually blind to see it. For instance, while proofreading this book, there were errors hidden in plain sight but since I'm not fully knowledgeable in grammar, I missed what was in front of me the whole time. My level of understanding determines my level of sight. The more we engage with God and know Him the more we will see that there is nothing to be afraid of. Everything with God is the truth and most of the things with man are theories.

Testing moments
Our enemy loves to attack our faith during testing time. They know that during most test God is quiet. Just like our natural teachers are quiet during a test so is God many times. Their goal is to have us feel inadequate during testing time. They want us to avoid our spiritual resources during the test. Every test we face in life is an open book test meaning we can always consult the word of God on how to answer a question but what the enemy does is to have us neglect Gods word and listen to the words of others. There is nothing to be afraid of when going through a test especially if God sent the test.

Let's look at some scriptures on fear.

1John 4:18 says, *there is no fear in love, but perfect love casts out fear. For fear has to do with punishment, and whoever fears has not been perfected in love.*

Love has a way of removing insecurities and fear. When a person feels like they belong to a group or a cause they become more of themselves. Wherever love is there is no fear. Think back to the most loving place you've ever been; did you feel afraid or insecure? I can bet you that you didn't. God's presence is full of love but our perspectives on ourselves and our situations must submit to that place. When you are in love there is no need to be afraid because love brings security. When you are assured that someone loves you, you don't have to worry about being abused or abandoned because they love you for you. Many of us have experienced fear in our relationships because that relationship was absent of true godly love. Never fall in love with a person that is not fully in love with God because if they are not in love with him they will not know how to love you. In order for us to eradicate the fear in others and create a culture of balanced love, we must know love as a noun. Before you can love as a verb you must know love as a noun. God wants you to be so close to him that he rubs off on you and you become an ELC an Express Love Centre for him so that when people are around you they will feel their fears being lifted. How close are you to Love?

The next part of the verse says that perfect love cast out fear. The key words in this verse is perfect love. God expressed his perfect love for us when he sent his son to live amongst us and to die for us. That expression of love sent ripple effects throughout time affecting us today. Because of what he did for us we no longer have to fear. We can face our mountains and engage in any situation with supreme confidence. Our confidence should never be in our ability alone but in Love being shown through our abilities. Christ confidence is key in casting our fear. No matter what situation I'm in I know that if he is with me whoever is against me is outnumbered. That is why we must stay in our word and in worship keeping our minds renewed. Fear is fake news we must learn how to weed it out so that we can see the facts in every situation. Now there is a difference between our facts and Gods facts. What you are facing now may be factual in time but is it factual in eternity? Your life has already been established and there is only one person that knows everything about it and that's God. If you stay close to him and follow him you will have no need to fear. Feeling overwhelmed by fear is proof that you haven't been immersed in God's love.

Understanding Gods love for us is a choice. Your current situation shouldn't outweigh the love of God in your mind. Nothing is greater than Gods balanced love for us. Keyword balanced. In order for his love to be perfect it must be balanced. Balanced meaning tender love and tough love. Gods greatest form of love is a love that restricts. True love is knowing what's best and what's not best for a person. That even during our crying, complaining, weeping and worrying he will do what's best for us. God's perfect love does that for us. His love is still love even when what we love is not present. God will not give you anything that will burden you. If he did, it would only lead you into a deeper place of fear and anxiety. It is our responsibility to have the right perspective on God's love and the only path that understanding is on is through the word of God. Not just reading it but allowing his word to marinate in our hearts. What marinating is to chicken is what meditation is to our hearts. We have to allow out hearts to sit in the seasoning of a passage until we become that passage. Chicken by itself is chicken but when it is in a BBQ Marinade it becomes BBQ chicken when it is in a cilantro lime marinade it becomes cilantro lime chicken. The chicken becomes what it is sitting in. The same is with our hearts when our hearts are marinated in love it becomes love when it is marinade in joy it becomes joyful. Who is your chef? Because whoever he is will determine what you will taste like.

Being perfected by God's love eliminates the desires to procrastinate and to be afraid. It leads to progression. We go hard for those we respect and truly love. The reason why many people don't go hard for God is because they haven't been perfected by his love. When you know how deeply you are loved and how undeserving you are of being in a relationship with God, you will do what he says that is why Jesus said if you love me, you would keep my commandments. True love is restricted love. People always say I don't believe in religion I have a relationship with God. You need both for a healthy relationship with God. Just like vows provide the boundaries for a marriage so does religion for our relationship with God. I'm not talking about religion made by man were talking about the commandments of God. If you love Him you will keep. Love helps us to keep. If you love your wife or husband then when you are away you are committed. True commitment is proven when you are away from your companion. The beauty of the cross is that we don't have to wait to walk with God in the cool of the day he is within us wherever we go. I'm so thankful that God sent Jesus who sent the comforter to be with us reminding us of what true love is. Now we can address what needs to be addressed and advance in life. Don't you want to see who you are in him don't you want to experience the plans God has for you? None of us in God should be afraid because we know who is with us. The bible says why fear or respect man who can only kill the body but cannot kill the soul? It says that we better fear the one who can put both body and soul in hell. This is not to scare us but to establish a serious principle that Gods words should trump any others. That if he says you can do it, then he will send the support and the security you need to see it through.

Here are some core symptoms of a stronghold or a soul tie to fear –

- fear of people,
- fear of authority,
- worry,
- anxiety,
- fearing the worst,
- being a copy,
- doubt and unbelief.
- procrastination
- always making excuses
- avoiding
- never prepared
- continuously missing opportunities

Now let's talk about some core solutions when it comes to fear. Number 1 - God is with us. **Isaiah 41:10** says, *Fear not for I am with you. Be not dismayed for I am your God, I will strengthen you, I will help you. I will uphold you with my righteous right hand.* I love this scripture because it tells us to fear not. *Fear not* is a command, every time you see words like that God is saying 'I am capable and I am confident in making these commands because I am confident in my ability. If I command you not to fear it is because I'm confident in my ability to help you through your fears.' The reasoning is because he is with us. You and I do not have to fear a thing simply because he is with us and if he is with us he will sustain us.

The next thing it says is that he is our God. *Fear not for I am with you, be not dismayed for I am your God.* He makes it personal. The reason why you should not be afraid of what you are afraid of is because God said, "Not only am I the God of the universe, but I am your God." He makes it personal; he also makes us a promise he says that he will strengthen us, help us and uphold us with His righteous right hand.

I love when it says, "I will uphold you with my righteous right hand." His righteous right hand stabilizes and secures us. Whenever the Bible talks about a right hand its talking about the strongest ability. Each of us have a strong hand, and that strong hand is the stronger of the two because of its ability to write, shoot a basketball etc. the imagery that God is trying to paint for us here is that he is able to do anything and that we don't have to worry about that hand stealing from us, abusing us or touching us inappropriately his hand has pure intentions. What or who is holding you today? I hope its God because he is the only one that can truly strengthen, help and hold us.

Deuteronomy 31:6 says, *Be strong and courageous, do not fear or be in dread of them, for it is the Lord your God who goes with you. He will not leave you or forsake you.*

Who are the people that are intimidating you? Whoever they are this verse lets us know two things that one you shouldn't be and two God sure isn't. God says for us to be strong and to be courageous and not to fear them because he is with us and will not forsake us. There is a land and a seat where you and I were commissioned to manage and right now in that land are giants and in that seat is a temporary king. We are commanded to be strong and courageous and not to fear them. There are two groups of people that intimidate us the most giants and temporary leaders. Giants in our land symbolizes people and voices that are keeping us from occupying our land. Joshua and Caleb were spies and amongst their troop were other spies telling the people that we are not able to take the land because in the eyes of the giants we are as grasshoppers; their perspective of the giants were bigger than their perspective of the God who said it was their land. However, Joshua and Caleb saw things differently they said that they were well able to possess the land. Which spy are you going to follow?

Temporary kings are rulers or overseers that are currently occupying our seats. I call them seat warmers. Many people are intimidated by the different rulers within society whether it be in music, Christianity, politics etc. David had this happen to him. Imagine hearing that the king selecting prophet is coming to your house to select the next king of Israel and that when he got there, your own father didn't allow you to be present. Imagine seeing the prophet coming to you and saying that you are the next king of Israel but after hearing those weighty words you had to go right back into your father's field, the one that didn't see you fit to be king and tend the sheep. Imagine helping the current king in battle and with music and then being forced away from that king because of you being a threat to him. That would really make you question if you were called to that place but he was. After a few years, he was king. I don't care who is occupying your seat just be thankful that they are keeping your seat warm and make sure that when you do sit in that seat of power that you don't misuse it. Why be intimidated by giants and temporary kings? God says to be strong and courageous and know that if God is not intimidated then neither should you. Whats causing you to be nervous what's causing you to lack courage? Once you answer those questions, really take some time and ask yourself which one is bigger; them or God?

His peace eliminates anxiety. You can't have his peace without his presence. In order for me to eliminate anxiety I have to be anxious to be in his presence. **Philippians 4:6-7** says, *Do not be anxious about anything, but in everything by prayer supplication with thanksgiving let your requests be made known to God and the peace of God which surpasses all understanding will guard your hearts and your minds in Christ Jesus.*

Before I continue let me make sure I make this plain, there is nothing wrong with feeling anxious, but executing in anxiety is where the sin is. Every unknown place, God knows you're going to feel anxious. Before I get married I'm going to feel anxious, before I have children there is going to be some anxiety, when it's time to get a house, when it's time to get a building for my ministry there is going be some anxiety. But the sin is not in feeling anxiety or feeling anxious; the sin is falling into it and allowing that anxiety to make you immobile. It is a command; he says do not be anxious about anything. He says there is nothing on this earth with me on your side that should paralyze you due to anxiety. He doesn't mind you feeling anxious for the first three or four minutes, but he is bothered when the anxiety last three to four weeks. Our mind should be so renewed in every area that when anxiety creeps in we will know how to process it in a matter of minutes. Now we must never forget that sin leads to anxiety. When you are in sin you will be anxious. Sin separates us from God and from doing what God wants us to do. When we are separated, we begin to trust in those sinful habits or sinful people and when we have had our full we begin to feel the weight of the sin and then begin to feel anxious seeing that those sinful habits and sinful people are incapable of helping us. Sin may be able to assist you for a few steps but it will not be there to help you through the long hall.

The next part of the verse says *but with everything by prayer and supplication with thanksgiving, let your requests be made known to God.* It says 'but in everything', everything you feel anxious about he says bring that to me. He says in everything that you feel anxious about communicate it with me, talk to me about it, petition to me about it, seek me about it. But make sure with that prayer, with that seeking, with that discouragement, with that fear, you come in with thanksgiving. When you make all your request known to God with thanksgiving, it gives you the right perspective, meaning that yes God I had a bad day, this bothers me, I'm afraid about the house, I'm nervous about getting married. God,

what is your will for me in this area? But if you only go to God with petitions and concerns but you never come with Thanksgiving then you will be unbalanced in your prayer time. But when you come into prayer with Thanksgiving you're telling God, "You know what, thank you for life, thank you for air in my lungs, thank you for giving me the ability to walk." But you may say, "Well Josh I only have one leg." Well instead, say "Thank you God that I'm able to see." "But Josh, I'm blind." Well instead, say "Thank you, God that I am able to feel." "Well Josh I have no arms." Well instead, say "Thank you God that I'm not in hell."
No matter what you are going through, there is always something to be thankful for. In addition, when you go into the presence of God where there is peace that peace will eliminate your anxiety, and your thanksgiving will balance out your petitions. No matter what you are going through there is always someone going through something worse and if you feel you are going through the worse of all worse on earth know that there is someone eternally damned in hell. Perspective is everything.

Every time you make your requests known to God you are guaranteed to receive something. You may not immediately receive what you are praying for, but you will immediately receive his **peace**. God isn't always going to give you what you've been asking for immediately, but he will give you his peace immediately. And what does his peace do? I'm glad you asked; His peace affirms that he heard and has handled your request; not always how you want it, but he has it handled. We must always remember that God is not Amazon with Amazon prime. Asking God for something is not like placing an order online with shipping dates etc. It's not we order, and then we determine the shipping its we order and then we trust that it will be shipped at the right time. With God we order, and he determines the shipping time. Trust His timing.

God's peace gives you security. There is nothing more comforting than knowing that heaven heard me. However, do not only let heaven hear what is worrying you or what is holding you down; let heaven hear that you are still thankful. The Bible says and the peace of God, which surpasses all understanding, will guard your hearts and your minds in Christ Jesus. His peace will ease all misunderstandings and cares and will guard your hearts and minds through what was done through Christ Jesus. That peace surpasses all understanding. Have you ever been in a situation where you still didn't get the answer, God didn't speak but you sensed it in your spirit that it was taken care of? That means that peace is letting you know it's handled, that peace is letting you know He heard. And why do we need this peace to guard our hearts and minds? That peace stabilizes the rushing thoughts that come into our minds like a river. It eases the emotional current that tries to rough up against the rocks of our hearts. It eases that. That's why thanksgiving is important, because when you hear what you are thankful for it reminds you of how faithful God has been to you.

Write down below all of your petitions or prayer request and beside them I want you to right down a praise or something you are thankful for. Once you have done this take some time and go before God in prayer and with every petition attach a praise or thanksgiving to it.

Prayer Request	Praise Release

Matthew 6:25-34 talks about not being anxious about your life, what you will eat or what you will drink, nor about your body or what you will put on. Is not life more than food and the body more than clothing? He also talks about looking at the birds of the air, they neither sow nor read nor gather into barns, and yet your heavenly father feeds them. Are you not more valuable than they? It also talks about which of you by being anxious can add a single hour to his span of life and why are you anxious about your clothes. He says consider the lilies of field. Basically, what this verses is telling us is that we don't have to worry about being anxious because if God can provide for the raven, he will provide for us. But what's so significant about the raven? The significance is that the raven was an unclean bird, and the people in that day knew about the uncleanness of the raven. That raven was a flesh-eating bird and if you touched that bird you become unclean. And Jesus was saying," Listen, listen. If God is able to even feed the "unclean" and provide for the "unclean", then surely he will provide for his children." When you know that about your God it eases all anxiety.

1 Peter 5:6-7 says *Humble yourself therefore under the mighty hand of God so that at a proper time he may exalt you, casting all your anxieties on him because he cares for you.*

We were never meant to carry our cares; we were told to cast our cares onto God. The reason why many of us are not progressing is because we're holding on to our cares and the reason why we get anxious at times is because we're not humble. Sometimes God has to humble us in order for us to cast our cares, because he knows that carrying our care will cause burnout. Notice we are not to hop on top of Gods knuckles but to humble ourselves up under his palms. He is the one that should dictate our promotions not us. For years we go to God and say; God, when is it my time? When is my moment? When will I no longer live in poverty? When will I no longer be in this situation? God, when will you get me out of this?" And he says, "Don't worry in my due time I will exalt you." Your due timing to a degree is predicated on your preparation. If you take care of your dues at this level, you will be prepared when your due time comes. Humility is key to success. Every room you enter in you should seek to be the lowest in the room knowing that everyone has something to teach you. Notice the scripture doesn't make the humbling process God's responsibility it says humble yourself under the mighty hand of God. It is wise to crawl up under the mighty hand of God because we know that hand provides safety. It provides safety from intruders, from sin and from ourselves; that while we are up under his hand we are comforted that his hand is moulding us, sheltering us, and keeping us. We should move based on the hand of God. The good thing about this passage is that it tells us that the same hand that we are under is the same hand that we will be over when its time to be exalted. It's important to stay still under his hand. So many of us get mad at God because his hand is restricting us. It's pointless to argue with God because when you are his and he knows that he has your heart you will, during the beginning stages, try and run from under his hand. You will run to the left and hit his thumb you will run to the right and bump into his pinkie finger you will try to run forward and bump into his pointer finger but he knows that overtime you will digress and trust him. God shields you because he knows you are not ready for the promotion. But when it is your time the same hand that is shielding you will swap up under you and raise you up. What we miss is that both positions are positions of protection. When you are under his hand you are protected and when he promotes you are protected. When he promotes you, he raises you high enough so that one, no one can get to you and two, that you respect the height enough to stay in his palm and not try and go to the edge. Those who humble themselves under Gods hand will be able to handle the heights of his promotions. Never forget that when God exalts you that is a high place, and you've got to make sure that you are humble first so that you won't become prideful when he exalts you. Because God knows if I exalt you and you are not humbled then you will walk off my hand and plummet to a spiritual death. That's why it's important for us to allow God to humble us.

When all else fails trust and seek.

Psalms 34:4 says *I sought the Lord, David said, and he answered me and delivered me from all my fears*. When all else fails you've got to trust and seek the Lord until you get an answer. The beautiful thing about what David was trying to tell us was that when he sought God, he was delivered from all his fears. God will if you let him deliver you from all your fears. He is the only one that knows how.

Fear is not from God.

2 Timothy 1:7 says *for God gave us a spirit, not of fear, but of power, love and self-control*, or another text says, *a sound mind*. Anytime you feel afraid longer than five minutes that fear is not natural, that fear is demonic. Any fear that you feel within the first thirty seconds to five minutes, that's normal. However, any fear that goes beyond those five minutes is now either an established fear complex or demonically suggested. Anything that is not from God you shouldn't want. It says for God gave us a spirit, not of fear, but it says that the spirit he gave us

through Christ's death, burial and resurrection was a spirit of power, love and a sound mind.

These three things are the three things that combats fear - power, love, and self-control. Fear sometimes makes you feel powerless, but when you are, embolden with power, you will walk in faith in every fearful situation. He gave you his spirit of love that corrodes lust and hate. It takes a lot of faith to love and to be long-suffering. Love is not for the weak in heart. He also gave you a spirit of self-control. Fear wants you to hide under pornography, under sex, under drugs, and under addictions, and not establish self-control. It is easy to start an addiction but it is hard to overcome one but with God, anything is possible.

To overcome the stronghold of fear you must build your faith. If your faith is small your execution will be small. Therefore, the best way to uproot and to untie these soul ties and strongholds is to establish a place where you can build your faith. Your faith = your trust and the best way to build you faith is to be faithful to the things of God. Utilize the prayer and the plan below to break your stronghold or tie to fear.

Fear and Procrastination					
How strong is the tie or hold in this area? →			Weak	Mild	Strong
Which areas are affected and in what way? Place a check beside each area that's affected and explain in what way in the larger box below.					
Spiritually	Mentally		Emotionally		Physically

Prayer:

Heavenly Father in the power of your son's name Jesus I come against every fearful situation in my life, every fearful emotion, every fearful thought, I curse it at the root in Jesus' name. I repent for entertaining fear and for procrastinating on my purpose. I am no longer afraid; I am full of faith. From this day forward, I will build my faith daily, I will build my faith in good times, I will build my faith in bad times, and I will build my faith in indifferent times. Heavenly Father, I thank you right now that your spirit will lead me into places that my faith will be stretched and strengthened. Thank you, Father for taking me into the unknown. Thank you, Father, for stretching me for I know that you are strengthening and developing my faith for a purpose.

Right now, I come against every demonic spirit of fear that's creeping in and around my life. I command you to go; I command you to never come against me again. I am now a house of faith; I am now a person of faith and every situation that I'm facing I will move forward in because I know my Heavenly Father is with me. I command every plot and scheme to be cancelled in the name of Jesus!

Thank you, Father, for being with me, for strengthening me and for upholding me. I thank you for increasing my faith today, helping me to go and step over what was once a mountain, but through you changing my perception, is now a molehill. I curse every type of spirit and plot of the enemy that is going to cause me to be afraid. I am no longer afraid; I am full of faith. I am no longer afraid; I am full of faith. I am no longer afraid; I am full of faith in the matchless name of Jesus. Amen!

Faith Builders Plan

I want you to list below the areas you desire to grow your faith and I want you to
develop a Faith workout plan utilizing the weights below. Write down a simple
plan you can stick to by answering the questions and within each day place a
check mark on when you plan to do each exercise. I'll give you a months' worth
of check points to help you plan it out. Treat this exercise like you would a regular
workout plan. Faith is a muscle and like any muscle it must be stretched and tested
for it to grow. Follow through the boxes below and develop your Faith workout
plan.

Weights: (Challenges)
   1. Meditating on God's Word
   2. Prayer and Praise
   3. Meeting with your accountability
   4. Fasting
   5. Engaging in community
   6. Working on your purpose projects
   7. Serving

In what areas would you like to increase your faith			
1			
2			
3			
Scriptures to meditate on for →	Area #1	Area #2	Area #3

Prayers to pray for →	Area #1	Area #2	Area #3

List Your Accountability and how they can help you in each area.

What do you need to potentially fast from to help you with each area?

Who is all in your community and how can they support you in these areas?

What are those things you have been putting off that could really help you be productive and increase your faith? (Books, songs, business ideas etc.)

Where could you serve weekly or monthly to inspire you to help the world in your own unique way?

Write the number(s) of the weight(s) you plan to do each day and utilize the larger box to journal your process.

	MON	TUE	WED	THU	FRI	SAT	SUN
W1							

Week 1 Reflection

	MON	TUE	WED	THU	FRI	SAT	SUN
W2							

Week 2 Reflection

	MON	TUE	WED	THU	FRI	SAT	SUN
W3							

Week 3 Reflection

	MON	TUE	WED	THU	FRI	SAT	SUN
W4							

Week 4 Reflection

What growth have you noticed in Area #1	What growth have you noticed in Area #2	What growth have you noticed in Area #3

CHAPTER FIVE – ABANDONMENT AND VOIDS

Voids are empty spaces.

Many of us were brought up with voids, some of us grew up in unbalanced homes –where we had no father or mother or if we did, they were not always present. A lot of us grew up in situations where we had no full provisions and it is affecting us tremendously now. A void of any kind can build a stronghold. God's original design was for us to have everything that we need to grow into maturity. Everything before the fall was provided even the ability to choose. But when we chose against God we fell into imperfection and within any imperfection there will be a chance we will be without. No one not even Jesus grew up in perfect conditions. Mary and Joseph weren't rich shoot they weren't even 16. Nobody has everything they need and even if they do without God, there is still a void. Our enemy preys on our vulnerabilities. He preys on the areas where we are lacking repetition meaning strength and relationship. He knows that the best way to conquer you is not to attack you where you are strong but where you vulnerable and immature. There are two seasons where you are the most vulnerable with Satan, and that is when you were a child and when you are a new Christian. He loves to prey on us when we are still learning the basics or are in situations we cannot control. His goal is to tackle you when you are growing up. That is why he is after the home structure and the church structure. These two structures are the main pillars of society if both are struggling then anyone growing up under them will suffer. He wants the fathers out of the home he wants mother's burden with work he wants other people with issues living under the same roof as you. He wants your pastor to be without accountability and under reproach, he wants you surrounded by unlearned and un-disciplined individuals because he knows those environments will not help fill the voids but deepen them. He loves structural damage in these areas because he knows how much we need them to mature.

The Four Major Voids.

Parental Voids

Some of us grew up in households where there was no father and/or no mother, causing deep wounds. There is a big difference between being raised by a woman and a man in a house vs. being raised by a mother and a father in a home. Let's break down the definition of a father and a mother. A father by definition is one who instructs, and a mother by definition is one who nurtures. A father is one by the best of his ability and by the help of God present to instruct a child through all if not most key stages of their life from crawling to fulfilling their purpose. A mother is one who by the best of her ability and by the help of God present to nurture a child through all if not most key areas of their life. Society has caused a strain on the family structure. We are now even at a place where people are not sure of what gender they are. Somewhere throughout time we lost the meanings of the words boy, girl, man, woman, husband, wife, father mother. Each of these words have meaning and describes a certain level of maturity. Our world right now is full of little boys and little girls trying to be what they are too immature to be. Despite our upbringings, God still requires understanding and maturity before entering a new phase of life. While God wants us to move off patience, Satan wants us to move off pulses. Pulses that pushes us into places we are not mature enough to handle causing us to be intoxicated with enjoyment not knowing that all fun comes with consequences. Sex feels good, but sex is much more than a feeling it is a function that conceives a child and when sex happens during a season where there is no maturity then the cycle repeats.

Imagine where our world would be today if we just did everything God's way? Imagine if boys grew into men first and from there added within their repertoire husband qualities before they pursued a woman so that when he does he will be ready to tailor his husband traits to his specific woman. Every step matters and when we skip steps we only create more structural damage to our family trees. That's why it's important to be honest with ourselves and to be aware of our lack of understanding. Its ok to sit out of a relationship for another year and take some time a way to really grow. You don't have to let the pressures of culture rush you into another relationship and you know you have issues inside. We repeat cycles when we don't create new positive ones. I saw it in my life
I grew up for the bulk of my life without a father. And so as I got older I didn't realize that a void was being created in me, that the way I viewed life wasn't balanced, the way I experienced life was trial an error; I didn't have instruction. The absence of a father in the home led to the roll switch of my mom; she was then pressured to provide the instruction which led to a lack of nurturing at times. I found myself looking for that nurturing in relationships and friends not knowing that during my dating years and building friends that it's not fair to them to fill that hole in my heart that only God could. I even found out that not having that instruction birth insecurities in my heart effecting how I lead that instead of trusting my natural leadership abilities I would look for others opinions hoping they would low-key lead me. This thing is deep, and Satan knows it. He knows the unbalance a lack of one (mother/ father) will cause. I've talked to tons of people

that are completely unaware of the effects of their parental voids. They walk through life trying to prove to their parents that they can or are wilting under the pressures of their demands. See many people have both parents but their parents are too protective causing their children to sacrifice themselves to live the life their parents wished they could. The beautiful thing about God is that he is the only piece that can fit into any unstable situation. He is the only one that can equally fill the parental void that was missing. He did it with me. Over the years I had to repent to God about the hurt and bitterness that I allowed to reside in my heart due to not understanding his will. I use to for years get mad at God about why I did not have a dad present at home. I use to envy my sisters and brother because my dad had remarried in Africa and had other kids with his new wife and stayed with them. I use to get mad in my early teenage years when he would reference my little brother as junior. I use to even harbour resentment towards my mom because she had to be tough raising a boy by herself and God had to show me my heart and let me know that Josh I was there the whole time. He opened my eyes to show me all the people he placed around me to be his hands and his feet to help guide me unscathed. He opened my eyes to show me that my mom and dad are humans but that they loved me and did the best they could.

I heard a person say that 89% of parenting is attendance. The enemy knows that if I can get a parent not to be in attendance at the awards show, in attendance at the play, in attendance at the dining room table, or in attendance when that break up happens, or in attendance when that hurt happens, or in attendance when anything bad happens, then the enemy can use that situation to cause a stronghold. All he has to do is make sure that the parent is not in attendance emotionally, spiritually and physically. Not having either can dramatically affect a child but God can dramatically use this dysfunction to shape you and show you who had perfect attendance through it all.

A lot of people have struggled with abandonment issues because their parents abandoned them. The good thing about the gospel is that no matter who abandoned you Christ came to fill that void. The beautiful thing is now my father, and I are great to this day and I no longer carry any of the residues, to the best of my knowledge, of a parental void, because God has really shown up to be that father and has brought my natural father and I closer. We must never forget that God sometimes removes some of these people because he knows their influence will cause you to be inactive in what he wants you to be to only in due time rekindle what was once removed.

Moms Name:
Dads Name:
Or Guardians Name:

What kind of relationship did you have with each parent or guardian or in other words how was life being raised by them?

Mom	Dad

What potential voids were caused during your upbringing and how are they affecting you now?

In what ways could you see God being present during it all and how could his faithfulness help you forgive your parents?

Peer Voids

Many people are struggling with the effects of not having solid friendships. We all need friends and one of the best qualities of a friend is evident in the root word end. We need people that will support us to the end. There are four circles you need to have in your life to avoid the effects of a peer void; you need

1. The circle that authored you
2. A circle above you,
3. A circle around you, and
4. A circle that admires you.

The circle that authored you is the creator aka the Godhead (the father, the son and the Holy Spirit). This circle is the most important circle in your life. This circle created you and knows you more than any other person on this planet and this Godhead desires to be your closest friend. God loves you and knows what is best for you. It is very important that you befriend God and let him lead you to your other support groups; if not you will end up misguided, neglected or cheered in the wrong direction.

The circle above you are your champions they are the people who are your mentors they are the ones that have conquered the enemies you are currently fighting. They are the ones who have a proven work ethic and faithfulness to God that is evident not just in their public life but in their private one as well. These individuals will help you navigate the storms and pressures of life. You need to ask God to show you or send you individuals who can disciple you and assist God in shaping you into the image of Jesus.

You also need a circle that is around you. These individuals are your comrades they are the people that are within your inner circle. They are the ones that are not too productive to check in with you like your mentors may be but are your boys or your girlfriends that are fighting the good fight of faith with you and that are able to sharpen you more on a daily/ weekly basis. They are not perfect, but they are bearing the fruit of progression and are motivating you daily to keep going forward. These individuals need to be either right at your level or a little bit above and are truly serious about pursuing God.

You also need a circle that admires you. These are what I call your carriers they are those you mentor or disciple. These ones carry your pearls and learn from you on how to follow God. You are their champion in Christ you need these individuals because God will use them to help you not fall into certain sins that could hurt them. Not too many people are champions though, so they fall into sins and hurt those that are following them. This is not to imply that you should be perfect; just passionately progressing after God to such a degree that you always remain above reproach. You are going to make mistakes, but you shouldn't make certain ones if you are a champion in Christ. Champions don't make rookie mistakes. Every rookie needs a vet. They need a veteran who can say "don't be nervous I've been through this before and you will ok" or "I use to struggle with that and here is how I was able to overcome it." No one who practices sin can truly help someone out of the sin they are practicing. Only those that are free can free others!

To succeed you need these four circles in your life. You need the Godhead as your best friend; leading and guiding you into all truth. You need sent mentors to help support the leading of the Godhead in your life. You need comrades to help sharpen you on a daily to weekly basis and you need admirers to keep you humble and focused on the great commission. None of these circles should have more than three individuals in them. The more you have in each group the more you can become confused. Keep each circle tight and be cautious in who you allow into these circles. Let God make the perfect circles.

You may not have these four circles evident in your life right away but if you are saved you will have the most important circle in your life; the Godhead and if he is present he will send you, in due season, the other circles. However, know that you will need all four eventually in your life to help you grow. And as you grow with God he will send them but before he sends them he will first bring you to himself to establish you and shape you so that when these others begin to show up in your life you will be committed to the Godhead first.

Utilize the four circles below to list your support groups and if you don't have any one in any of these areas make sure to pray to God to fill these areas. And never forget; let your creator hand select who goes in each circle.

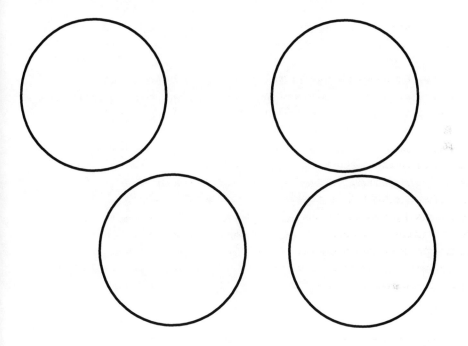

Pain Voids

People create pain voids by not addressing what needs to be addressed. Pain is necessary for you to be successful and for you to be successful;

- you must embrace your pain,
- become educated about your pain and
- execute from your pain.

Many people make excuses about their pain instead of embarrassing it. Imagine, where you would be today if you would have embraced what happened to you at 7, 16 or 28? Imagine the poverty you could have overcame by now or the relationship that could have been rekindled by now if you would have just simply embraced whatever caused you so much pain. So many people fail to realize just how great of a resource their pain is. The quicker you embrace it and educate yourself about it the closer you will be to executing from it. Many people right now have a void in their life because they were unwilling to address their pain. But you've heard this saying before, 'no pain, no gain'. Nothing grows in comfort zones, you've got to be uncomfortable, you've got to go through pain to be successful. And if you are afraid of pain then you will always create voids in your life and you will always create the void of 'what if.' 20 years from now, you are either going to regret the decisions you are making now or rejoice in the decisions you're making now. I want to be 77 years old, sitting on my wrap-around porch in the country, with no regrets. I rather go through the pains of progression and preparation now than to avoid them and suffer years later with "I wish I would have".

Do not mismanage your youth or your current opportunity to embrace your pain. God will never lead you beneath, above, or around your wilderness, he will always lead you through it. Walking with God is painful, but the rewards are plentiful. Who cares if it's painful if God is with you? And yes, God is going to inflict pain and allow you to go through things, that's the nature of life, but pain is what strengthens you. Many people retreat at the feeling of resistance, but you shouldn't retreat when you feel resistance, you should keep reaching forward, because every person who works out knows resistance makes you stronger. If you can lift it easily, there's no strength. Anytime you feel it getting easy in any area of your life you must add an extra plate to it, you must feel the pain because the pain lets you know that you've levelled up. I heard someone say that when you break a bone that bone when it heals becomes stronger. Let the break happen because when God breaks you, you will heal back stronger. But you won't become stronger if you try to avoid the breaking or become impatient and negligent during the healing process. See, God is going to break you whether you like it or not. God is going to lead you through some things that is going to break the pride, lust, and jealousy off you so that when you stand on the platforms He has for you the temptations won't break you. See Jesus didn't go from the lake where he was baptized to preaching in Galilee; he went from the water to the wilderness to be tested, to be pruned and to be prepared. If you can't pass the test in the wilderness what makes you think you will pass the test when you're out there working for God? God must break what will be a liability to what he wants you to build. What are you avoiding? What do you need to address today? Are you running away from the pain or embracing it?

What are you avoiding that needs to be addressed and why?

What do you need to do to address or embrace your pain?

What could your pain be teaching you?

Preparation Void

Another void is the lack of preparation. Success happens when opportunity meets preparation. Many of us are creating voids in our lives or are missing opportunities because we are not prepared. You've got to ask yourself, "What am I willing to prepare for?". God is not just a promoter he is also the one that prepares. Many believers want to be promoted but are not willing to be presented prepared. John the Baptists mission statement was to present to God a people prepared. I too adopted this mission; I want to present to God a people prepared to be used by him. Everyone is present during promotion messages but become silent or distant when it is time to learn how God prunes.

These voids manifest themselves when people try to pursue what they are too immature to manage. God is not going to promote you in any area you are not fit to manage. God is looking for managers and overseers. He is looking for people who are willing to put the work in. Your worth is to a degree predicated on your work ethic. Things work together for those that are willing to work hard. When you worship, work, and war hard you will win hard. Are you willing to put the work in or not? The bible says those that faint in the day of adversity, their strength will be proven small (Proverbs 24:10). Adversity is going to come, and those that prepare in the presence of God will be able to stand. If you are not willing to stand in the presence of God, you will not be able to withstand what's coming ahead. What opportunities are you missing today because you are too lazy to prepare? What voids are in your life right now because you are not willing to work. If you work hard now you will be able to play hard later.

***

The enemy understands that the best way to cause a person to be stifled is to cause them to always reflect on who left. I can be personal right now; abandonment was probably one of the top things that I had to wrestle with in my life. Throughout many years of my life, I knew more people who left than who stayed, that may not be the truth, but it sure felt like that. And I used to wrestle with that because I would begin to hold on to everything, I became a hoarder. I didn't want anybody to help me because I was afraid they were going to leave. There were points in my ministry where I set up the camera; I set up the tables; I didn't want to delegate anything because I thought if I delegated to you, you would leave eventually, and I would be left alone again so why not do everything. But when I begin to understand that it doesn't matter who comes and goes and that God will always be faithful to me; I began to trust more. It doesn't matter who comes and goes in your life, if God brings them there, they will serve their purpose.

Now I'm sure there are going to be sometimes when I'm probably going to struggle with this battle, but I'm thankful that God is healing me. From the author to the reader, everyone has an area they struggle in, but God is able enough to help you. If I can progress beyond my abandonment issues and become stronger and better equipped, then surely you can. I'm thankful that God will never abandon me, I'm thankful that God will never forsake me; it's comforting. Sometimes we focus more on who left than the ones and the One who didn't. Never seek closure from those who do not desire to give you closure. Embrace those that are close and forsake the need for closure from those that left. Many people are struggling with this area because they just want to know why they left. Don't worry about finding out why they left; they left.

Right now, I am confident in who I am because I know I'm one of a kind, and when you know you are one of kind, and people leave you, you count it as a loss for them and not a loss for you. I've noticed in ministry that when people get comfortable with me, I become common to them and they begin to treat me lesser now than how they did the first day they met me. That is why you must build some mystique about yourself; you can't show everything about yourself to everyone because not everyone can carry, comfort, challenge or correct you. Never forget; people who get too comfortable with you will forget what drew them to you in the first place. Always improve and add some mystique to your life.

Ps: I too had to learn that it's not always the person who left's fault; sometimes we play a part in people leaving too. It's not right to harbour abandonment feelings when you know you played a part as well. What I was talking about before is for when you see a pattern of people leaving for stupid reasons. I noticed in my life that there were people who left me, and I played a part and there were times where people left and I was confused on why they left. People leave for four reasons

1. one, you hurt them, and they can no longer be around you,
2. two, they have become offended and are too immature to approach you to save the friendship
3. three, God escorts them out of your life or
4. four, they no longer see value in you.

Either way, don't harbour any resentment towards them or yourself. If you played a part in hurting someone and you have reached out to them and have asked for forgiveness, but they still choose to leave then let them go and heal away from you. Those who have been hurt do not always want to go to the one that caused the hurt for healing. It is not wise for them too because the one that caused the hurt will suffer wounds while trying to heal. It is always best to heal separately (if you can) from the one who hurt you or whom you have hurt because either they will become a punching bag, or you will become a punching bag while the healing is taking place. If the person leaves because of offence and are not willing to approach you then they are not mature enough to be your friend. Friends who value each other will reach out to amend any wrongs. Some people make people into gods and when that person proves not to be God they get offended and leave.

This is true to the fourth point; people will hide behind the word offense to validate a reason to walk away from you because you are no longer valuable to them. Don't let people determine your value. People will leave you high and dry and you did nothing wrong and that's ok because those people will feel the effects of not having you around. Let leaches learn on their own when they leave. When you become common to people and you have lost your mystique; people leave you to find someone else to entertain them that's why its never wise to bring too many people close to you because not everyone can handle what comes with being close to you. Many people are drawn to you because of what they have noticed from a distant but when they get closer to you and you begin to show them that you are human or that you are not God their false expectations of you will cause them to exit out of your life. Stay consistent because those people will regret leaving you. I always tell young brothers that not everyone can be Jordan or Lebron meaning not everyone can increase the value of others. When others begin to play with you and begin to notice their points and overall play increasing because of you; don't get mad when those players want to see if they can do it without you. Let them leave because soon they will find out that not everyone can be a once in a lifetime calibre player. Let people feel what its like not to have you around all the time; don't always be so accessible because some people are only growing because of Gods work in your life and not off of what God wants to do in theirs. When these people leave don't allow their abandonment to cause your value to plummet causing you to mope around for months; instead, mop up the mess they left and keep going forward.

You don't want people to leave and come back with proof that leaving you was valid. You want to be seen improved so that when they come back they will notice that they missed out. Only time proves who truly won a breakup. Keep improving and know that not everyone who leaves; leaves on their own; sometimes its God escorting them out of your life. Some people God escorts completely out of your life and some he escorts out and then escorts back in, but I always tell people to never build a friendship with someone that is greater than your friendship with God because when you do you will always feel deeply hurt or borderline depressed if not depressed when they leave. In the beginning I would be out of the game for months because of an ex or a friend that left but now when people leave it barely affects me. But I too make sure that I don't give good people a reason to leave due to pride, ego, lust or straight up being irritable.

Here are some **core symptoms** of a person who struggles with abandonment and voids –
- they always feel the feelings of rejection,
- they always feel neglected,
- they always feel like a victim,
- they don't want to be intimate with anyone; not even with their spouse.
- they burn bridges easily
- they like to isolate themselves
- they begin not to value people and relationships anymore;
- they run away good people
- they overthink

Loneliness becomes a safe-haven and self-pity becomes their core emotion. When a person feels these types of symptoms, they struggle with abandonment. These people also don't want to share, they don't want to share anything about themselves, they become closed off. We need community to grow; we need others to go forward.

Let's talk about some **core solutions**. Number 1 - you've got to let God be the replacement.

You've got to let God replace what was removed; and if God removed it, he removed it for a reason. If it left, let it leave, because if it was meant for you, it would've stayed. My mom used to tell me that if a girl breaks up with you Josh, never accept her back because she should have known who she had in the first place'. You've got to be confident in who God has made you to be if not you will continuously be a revolving door for people.

Hebrew 13:5-6 says,

Keep your life free from love of money, and be content with what you have, for he has said, "I will never leave you nor forsake you." [6] So we can confidently say,

"The Lord is my helper;
    I will not fear;
what can man do to me?"

That's confidence, knowing that no matter what I go through, I know the Lord is my helper, why should I fear? What can anyone do to me? Just because a person leaves doesn't mean you're destroyed. Just because they leave doesn't mean you should cry about it for months; now it's ok to feel hurt because someone left; you're human, but don't continue to pick at that wound and not give it time to heal. That's why you've got to be confident knowing that life is more than money and about who or what is in your life. When you're more focused on the love of money and what you do or don't have, it will make you miss out on the fact that God will never leave you or forsake you. Money and people will leave but God will never leave.

Romans 8:38-39 says *for I am sure that neither death nor life nor angels nor rulers nor things present nor things to come, nor powers nor height nor depth nor anything else in all creation will be able to separate us from the love of God in Christ our Lord.*

That's powerful. Nothing on this planet can separate you from the love of God. People can come and go, things can fall apart, people can abandon you, but Romans says nothing can separate you from the love of God. Because of what Christ Jesus has done and because he's your Lord he will never let you down. Everybody else can leave you and abandon you, but he says neither death nor life nor angels nor rulers nor things present nor things to come, nor powers nor height nor depth nor anything else in all creation can separate you from His love. That's powerful. That's confidence, people may leave, you may feel alone; but God is with you. To overcome abandonment, you've got to make sure you anchor yourself in the fact that God will never leave you, that's important. Every day you have to remind yourself and say, "Thank you God for staying."

Soul ties and strongholds form through abandonment. None of us were born in a perfect home, no one can be a perfect friend, pain is not always easy to go through and always preparing for something can be annoying and that's ok. None of these holes can be filled or healed if we don't deal with the biggest hole in our hearts and that our need for a holy God. God is the only one who can solve any abandonment problem you have. You have to really go to God and be honest with him and let him in so that he can shine the lights in the areas where you are struggling. Which voids do you have?

Abandonment						
How strong is the tie or hold in this area? →				Weak	Mild	Strong
Which areas are affected and in what way? Place a check beside each area that's affected and explain in what way in the larger box below.						
Spiritually	Mentally		Emotionally		Physically	

Prayer:

Repeat the prayer below and progress beyond your abandonment.

Heavenly Father I thank you for always being there and for always being present. Even in your silence, I am a comforted by your presence. Heavenly Father, I repent for harbouring resentment and abandonment in my heart towards (list everyone you are harbouring resent for)

_____

_____

_____

_____ and

I forgive them for leaving me. I am completely letting them go out of my heart right now in Jesus' name. Because Father I know for a fact that you remove things to be the replacement. Heal my heart today of all bitterness, resentment, and un-forgiveness. Heal me God from the need of providing for my voids. God, I forgive my parents; I forgive those friends that may have left and I am thankful that you are helping me address my pains. Help me to prepare for my purpose.

Right now through the authority of Jesus Christ, I come against every demonic spirit that's keeping me feeling rejected. I am not rejected; I am received. I may have been rejected by others Satan, but I am received by God, and I receive his love for me, I receive his care for me, I receive it now in Jesus' name. I command every demonic spirit to leave my presence now, leave me now! Father I'm going to walk in my acceptance now and I'm letting go of all abandonment. I'm thankful that you adopted me, I no longer have to feel abandonment and I rest in that truth! Father continue to help me as I become freed from this. I know I have broken it in the spirit, but God help me to break it mentally, emotionally and physically. I love you Father! Amen!

Continue to use the exercises in this chapter and the previous ones to help you break the soul-tie or stronghold mentally, emotionally and physically.

CHAPTER SIX – GUILT AND SELF-HATE

One of the greatest tools demons use against us is condemnation. They lure us into a place of condemnation through temptations. The same voice that tempts you will be the same voice that condemns you. The same voice that cheers you into a place of sin is the same voice that will criticize and condemn you for being in it. Self-hate leads to neglect. When a person feels condemned they begin to hate themselves, they hate themselves either because of what happened to them or what they may have caused to themselves. Are you going through self-hate? Do you love you? Do you like you? Do you embrace every day that you are fearfully and wonderfully made? The devil doesn't want you to have self-love because self-love leads to self-help, and self-help leads to self-care. He understands that when you truly love yourself, in a balanced way, then you will take care of yourself. But if you hate yourself you will neglect yourself. A lot of people are drowning in the murky waters of condemnation; they're drowning because they don't believe that God can heal them. The devil knows that for any person to feel this way there must be a process. He wants to make sure that every nonbeliever doesn't come into the knowledge of Christ, and he wants to make sure that every believer doesn't know what Christ can truly do for them.

There are these six L's I want to talk about - longing, lust, look, lure, linger, latch; the process of drifting you into condemnation. For you to get into a place of guilt, self-hatred or condemnation the enemy has to build a longing. Where there's longing there's discontentment. A lot of people are not content with where God has them, therefore, they long for a companion; they long for more money, they long for a better house. The children of Israel did this; this is nothing new; they longed for a king. And the thing about God, God will often allow what you long for to come into your life. Because he wants to let you see that what you are longing for is incapable of sustaining you. Therefore, the devil begins to attack your perception of God. He will begin to make you believe that God is not enough; ask Eve. He began to tell Eve that this fruit would give her access to a mysterious wisdom that only God held. And so, she bought into the suggestion because she longed for that place, she longed for that position, and from that longing lust built. When you are content with God, love builds. When you are discontent with God, lust builds. Lust is an overbearing desire that will cause you to look outward. It will cause you to be lured by people or products to a place where you become addicted and the addiction will cause you to linger long enough until you are latched onto a way of thinking and living. Any way of life outside of God will cause you to be like the prodigal son; living a low life. A low life or a life outside of the presence of God will always affect your self-esteem and when your self-esteem is affected, you begin to hate yourself. The devil does not want you to care for you he wants you to fall into lifestyles that will at the end leave you with a mind full of guilt, shame and condemnation. You see he loves to utilize tailored temptations to take you away from your place of freedom, he knows what will cause you to leave God and he will lure you through your temptations into sins knowing that the sin will cause you to naturally feel condemned. Condemnation leads to guilt and guilt leads to self-hatred.

That same voice that said this will help you will laugh at you. I tell people when you feel condemned, or you feel guilty, run to a just judge, run to God like never before. Many people run away from God when they feel condemned and Satan loves it. God hears every sincere prayer that you pray, even if you made a mistake two minutes ago if you genuinely have remorse for it and you genuinely confess it he will forgive you. But before you confess you must be ready to let go.

The **core symptoms** of guilt and self-hatred are
- anger,
- shame,
- self-pity,
- inferiority,
- uneasiness,
- embarrassment,
- neglect
- withdrawal
- deep addictions
- suicidal thoughts
- fear
- avoiding the right kind of help
- adopt new sins
- run away from God
- always hating on others
- abusive

If you have any of these symptoms, then you may be struggling with guilt and self-hatred. Why don't you love you? Take some time below to write down what you like, love or hate about yourself and really write down why you feel this way about yourself. I also want you to write down the areas you have neglected and ways you can take better care of yourself in those areas.

What do you like/ love about yourself and why?	What do you dislike or hate about yourself and why?

What are the areas you have neglected due to self-hate or guilt?	In what ways could you take better care of yourself in these areas?

Next, **core solutions**. 1 John 1:9 says *if we confess our sins he is faithful and just to forgive us of our sins and to cleanse us from all unrighteousness.*

Confession is important; it opens the door to our cleansing. God is faithful to cleanse any sin if the sinner is faithful in confessing. Many people miss out on the opportunity to be cleansed because they don't either want to confess their sins or they are completely unaware of their unrepentant sins. Whatever we have yet to confess will be the very thing used against us either by demons or just through the natural effects of unrepentant sin. You've got to confess quickly because if you believe that God is true and you believe that Jesus lived, and is real then all you've got to do is confess your sins. Write down below the sins that you need to confess, and begin to tell yourself that I believe that he will be faithful to forgive me and to cleanse me. God will cleanse you but you have to let God do it. He is faithful and just.

What sins do you need to confess and what systems do you need to implement in your life to ensure you are truly done with those sins.

Sins to confess	Systems to overcome them. (Like who would you need to cut off or what new habits you will need to implement).

John 3:17 says, *For God did not send his Son into the world to condemn the world but in order that the world might be saved through him.* Jesus was not sent to condemn, and He doesn't seek to condemn. The whole purpose of God wrapping himself in flesh and being amongst us was not to say, "Hey, I'm perfect and you're not." He was coming to swap, he was coming to take your unrighteousness and give you his righteousness, he was coming to take your condemnation and to kneel and cleanse you. He was not sent to the world to condemn us but to save us. If you feel condemnation, then it is not from God. Jesus convicts but he doesn't condemn. Conviction will always precede condemnation; conviction will always precede a committed sin. The devil cannot beat God's conviction. God will always convict us of sin, but he will never condemn us for it. But you must have enough trust in God that when God convicts you about something you obey. Not only should we heed to Gods convictions we

must also appreciate his chastening. The Bible says that he chastens those he loves and remember what was said in Psalms 23 by David he said, "thy rod and thy staff they comfort me". Being chastened by God proves that you are a son and daughter of God and that he loves you. I love what David said even though to some it may be confusing. Some would say how can a whooping comfort me; whooping's hurt, this is true, but the rod and staff show that there is someone present in your life that cares enough to correct you and after years pass you will begin to appreciate the corrections of God. I am who I am because of the whoopings and the words of my mom and God!

Those who are mature in God will heed the convictions of God knowing that convictions will lead to predictions meaning in every conviction you can predict what will happen if you follow through with the sin. What helps me many times is that I think myself into trouble to keep myself out of trouble. I always think about what will be the fruit that will come out of this. Never let anything drown out God's convictions.

Romans 8:1 says, *there is therefore now no condemnation for those who are in Christ Jesus.* Man, it feels good to know that I am in Christ meaning I am in His saving work. I'm going through his sanctification soul wash and he is processing me. I don't have to feel bad about where I am in the various stages of sanctification because I am confident that I am in the right place and based on my cooperation the conveyer belt is steady pushing me through the cleaning cycles. It is important that we know what it means to be in Christ and how we should be patient with the process. Right now, erase the pressures of perfection in your mind. You can't handle that weight. You are going to mess up again and that's ok because God chose you with your future mistakes in mind. Its like a parent teaching their daughter or son how to ride their bike a good parent won't chastise their child if they fall because they know its expected even when they have mastered riding there may be a situation that will cause them to lose control and fall but we've all heard the saying that it is like riding a bike; once you have learned something and its in you its hard to let go. It's hard to unlearn how to ride a bike the same is with maturity in Christ when you make a mistake you just simply brush yourself off and get back on the bike and ride because you confident in the one who taught you how to ride. If God has chosen you and you are in Christ, then you shouldn't allow condemnation to affect you. Christ will never send you condemning thoughts so when you feel them trying to creep in your mind or heart take a moment to encourage yourself about who you are in and tell that demon that I am a son or daughter of God

Jesus brings conviction but never condemnation. You don't have to worry about ever being condemned; you don't ever have to worry about self-pity and self-hatred because your self-love was built on His love for you. Because of what Jesus did on the cross, we now can confess, and from our confessions, all condemnation can leave; that's freedom. You no longer have to be bound by condemnation, you right now can confess your sins and if you believe and trust that God is real, you will begin to feel the holy rag of God wiping those guilt and condemnations away.

Romans 3:23 says, *for all have sinned and fall short of the glory of God.* Everyone has fallen short and there is no sin God can't cleanse. All sins can be confessed, meaning there is no new sins under the firmament. Listen, there is no sin that God cannot cleanse; any sin can be confessed cleansed and corrected. We must everyday trust in the one who never sinned or fallen short of what was impossible for us to do. Do you really understand how high perfection is? No one can reach that mark but God that's why he came in the likeness of man to pay the price of imperfection so that we can be his light bearers and be the catalyst to set others free. This verse should help you breathe and know that one, no one is perfect and two stop trying to be perfect! You won't be perfect until after death so enjoy progressing throughout life and really slowing your life down and see and appreciate God working on you and through you.

James 4:7 says, *Submit yourself therefore to God, resist the devil, and he will flee from you.* To completely avoid condemnation, you must first be submitted under God. Listen, many of us, the reason why the devil hasn't left and the reason why we keep losing our battles is because we are not first submitted under God. When you're submitted to God, you will be more susceptible to be led by God. The enemy hates it when you are submitted and led by God because he knows he cannot win when God is present and appreciated. When you are completely committed and submitted to God, you can resist the devil. Being under God's leading is the safest and peaceful place you can be and once you have truly felt his presence, you will easily resist the devil. For example, it doesn't matter how much people brag about their potato salad or about how good it is; because of my experiences with it, I can easily resist it. I do not care if my resisting hurts the cook's feelings I am not going to appease their inquiry to go through another negative experience with potato salad especially when there are better options at the cookout. The same is with God when you know what it feels like to be in God's presence and what it is like to be out of it you will easily resist what Satan is cooking. However, you must always make sure you are surrounded by, to the best of your ability, a godly environment and you must make sure that old sins are not within arm's reach because it is hard to resist something over a long period of time that is continuously within arm's reach. You must rid it from being so close so that you can remain close to God.

1 Corinthians 10:13 - *No temptation has overtaken you that is not common to man. God is faithful, and he will not let you be tempted beyond your ability, but with the temptation will also provide the way of escape that you may be able to endure.*

There are no new temptations. For those that are submitted he is faithful not to let you be tempted beyond your ability. The beautiful thing about God is that with every temptation there is a way of escape. God always makes a way for us to not fall into temptation. Every time you are presented with a temptation you have a 30-second window to choose. The devil never brings temptations when you are at your strongest he brings temptations when you are at your weakest. He knows he has a better chance of causing you to fall when you have fallen away from God. He roams around to see what he can use to drift you from your strong place because he knows that if he can drift you from your strong place in God you will be more susceptible to buy into the temptation. Temptations become overwelming when we are at our weakest. We feel overtaken by them when we have been made weak overtime. Satan systematically makes us weak mentally. He sneaks things into our environment that will have a high percentage chance of causing us to compromise and to leave our position in God. Once we are away from our source for a long period of time one small temptation that we would of weeks ago easily tossed aside now becomes overwelming. We've all been there whether it was with an ex boyfriend/ girl friend or with a random. We were so sexually triggered and out of character that they ugly self lol caught us at a bad time and we fell into a sexual sin with them and once the sin was over we looked at them and was like why in the world did I waste my time. It wasn't even worth it; but at the time we thought that it was everything we needed. This happens all the time! Temptations are there heaviest when we are at our weakest and our weakest points are when we truly don't love ourselves. People with low self esteem will always settle and that's unfortunate. Do you feel overwhelmed when tempted? If so why?

Matthew 26:41 - *Watch and pray that you may not enter temptation. The spirit indeed is willing, but the flesh is weak.* The flesh is not capable of doing anything genuine or good, you cannot put any trust in the flesh (your sin nature) because your flesh is weak. Your spirit may be willing, but your flesh is weak. Whichever you feed most will lead most. We've got to make sure we understand that we cannot put any trust or food in the flesh. And the best way to not even entertain temptation is always to be watchful and prayerful. When you're always talking to God you begin to build discernment; you will be able to know the difference between what's good and what's bad for you.

Before I move on let me define what your sin nature is. Your sin nature is a part of you that is more inclined to sin than to win with God. You cannot win with habitual sin in your life. We are commanded to kill our flesh daily and we do that through starving it. For something to starve its food supply must be cut off. For your sin nature to die, you must ensure it does not receive any support. But for there to be no support, you must one, be aware of the sins you struggle with and two, how is this sin being supplied. Sin leads to self-hate especially for the believer because of the guilt that comes with it. Your flesh is not your body your flesh or sin nature is an inward disease that has contaminated your soul realm and your body realm aiming to continuously harbour old habits and thoughts that will keep the nature alive. That's why the Bible says that we are transformed by the renewing of our minds. If we think correctly we will see and live correctly! Our level of thinking will determine our level of discernment. Discernment is key to success because discernment will help you see what's not clear to others and when you know what's deeper you will be able to know how to move around temptations. Its amazing to know that we have a spirit in us that is always willing and ready and all we must do is just simply let it lead. What is leading you? Are you being led into temptation or around them?

James 1:12-16 - *Blessed is the man who remains steadfast under trial for when he has stood the test he will receive the crown of life which God has promised those who love him. Let no one say when he is tempted I am being tempted by God, for God cannot be tempted with evil, and he himself tempts no one. But each person is tempted when he or she is lured and enticed by their own desires. Then desire when it has conceived gives birth to sin, and sin when it is fully grown brings forth death. Do not be deceived my beloved brothers.*

Being steadfast proves commitment. The Bible says blessed is the man or person who remains steadfast under trial. The beautiful thing about it is that my commitment proves my level of steadfastness. The more I'm committed, the the longer I stand. The less I'm committed, the less likely I will stand. God never tempts. No one can ever say that God tempted them, because God cannot be tempted with evil and If God is not tempted with evil, he can never use evil to tempt us. God tests, but never tempts; the devil tempts, but never tests. The process of temptation is in the verse, it says you will be lured and enticed by your own desires. The devil understands the best way to lure you is through your own desires. And when those desires are born or at their peak they will birth sins - they will birth a sex addiction, a pornography addiction, an eating disorder it will birth all kinds of sins, it will birth greed addiction, money addiction, it will birth these different things. And when it is full grown, it will bring forth death. The demons assigned to you will follow their kingdoms mission statement which is to steal, kill and destroy and they will look for ways to put to death your purpose. If they can kill your purpose in your mind or bombard your life with the consequences of your sins, then you will depreciate in value to God. The enemy puts to death what God wants you to do by building perverted desires, because they know that if they can build a perverted desire or a perverted longing you will leave God and attach yourself to a sin. In addition, if he can keep you in this secular haven of manipulation and deceit, that sin will birth death. It will bring death to your marriage, ministry, business, name, and reputation and if they can get a hold of your name and reputation, they will taint your testimony! What are you allowing in your life? What sins are you allowing to grow? Be careful because with all sins death is imminent.

Hebrews 2:18 - For because he himself has suffered when tempted he is able to help those who are being tempted. Since Jesus passed his tests, we can pass ours because we have his help. We can't trust in our ability we have to trust in his ability through us completely!

The best way for the enemy to destroy your purpose is to have you hate yourself. Many people have allowed the various systematic forms of oppression to cause them to hate themselves. The enemy of joy is comparisons. So many people hate who they are due to what they do not have and due to who has what they would like to have. When we make comparisons, we rob ourselves of our uniqueness. Imagine how many people's true personalities are buried under their false personalities mimicking off what's trending. You will always lose value trying to be like someone else. God did not create you to be a copy he created you to be an original and the moment you embrace your originality in him the quicker you will begin to take care of you. Who are you comparing yourself to? Let the guilt go and grab a hold of Christ and let him set you free. Repeat the prayer below and really spend some time with God.

Guilt				
How strong is the tie or hold in this area? →		Weak	Mild	Strong
Which areas are affected and in what way? Place a check beside each area that's affected and explain in what way in the larger box below.				
Spiritually	Mentally	Emotionally	Physically	

Prayer

Father, I thank you for your love. I am so thankful that you didn't come into this world, let alone into my life to condemn me but to set me free. God help me to be strengthened and strong enough to trust your convictions. God help me to build such a thirst and hunger after you that I'll no longer have to long for anything that is displeasing to you. Father I believe in the power of the blood and of the cross and because of what you did on the cross for me I am completely liberated from guilt, shame, and condemnation Father, I repent for every sin that I have committed from this place of guilt. I repent of

----

----

 and I embrace my freedom now in Jesus name!

Right now, through the authority of Jesus, I come against the spirit of discontentment and guilt. I am content in God. I am in love with God and I no longer long for anything in this world above him. I cancel all of your plots and schemes now in Jesus Name! Father I turn my attention back to you and I thank you again for setting me free. I love you Father, Amen!

Self-Care Plan

What are the things you need to care for in your personal life?

Where would you like to see your self 1 to 3 months from now?

What must you do for you to meet those goals?

For the next 90 days I want you to just simply check the box of the day you took out time to care and improve you. Write your goals down and tackle them through self-love.

Month 1: Goals

D1	D2	D3	D4	D5	D6	D7	D8	D9	D10
D11	D12	D13	D14	D15	D16	D17	D18	D19	D20
D21	D22	D23	D24	D25	D26	D27	D28	D29	D30

Month 2: Goals

D31	D32	D33	D34	D35	D36	D37	D38	D39	D40
D41	D42	D43	D44	D45	D46	D47	D48	D49	D50
D51	D52	D53	D54	D55	D56	D57	D58	D59	D60

Month 3: Goals

D61	D62	D63	D64	D65	D66	D67	D68	D69	D70
D71	D72	D73	D74	D75	D76	D77	D78	D79	D80
D81	D82	D83	D84	D85	D86	D87	D88	D89	D90

CHAPTER SEVEN - HOLLOW WORDS

Trust is the hardest thing to build but the easiest thing to break. Trust must be managed and kept. Many people are living untrustworthy lives. They live a life online they don't live in real life; their public and private lives do not match. Trust is a very important thing to God and to others. We exchange ideas, currency, and a lot of things because of trust. And once trust has been broken it's hard to build it back.

There are three trusts that we need to maintain - God's trust, people's trust, our trust.

Let's talk about God's trust. God loves everyone equally but doesn't trust everyone equally. Every child of God is equally loved; but not every child of God is equally trusted. Can God trust you with treasure? Can God trust you with trouble? Can God trust you with time? If God can't trust you with these three things then your life will be stale and stagnant, but when you are proven to be trusted with treasure - treasure being money, treasure being the value of a person's heart - when you are trustworthy God can add more people into your life, God can add more treasure to your life. When God can trust you with trouble, then he knows he can trust you with more, because to whom much is given much is required (Luke 12:48). When he can trust you with trouble then he knows he can trust you during temptations. When God knows he can trust you with time he knows that you understand patience and are willing to allow her to have her perfect work. But when God can't trust you with those things you will miss out on a journey that he desires to have you on.

People's trust - we've got to make sure we manage and keep the trust of people. In ministry right now, I must make sure I keep people's trust, I've got to make sure I live above reproach, I've got to make sure I practice what I preach. Because I know that if I fail in my commitments then it can negatively affect people's commitment to God, because babes are babes, when someone of a stronger statute does something wrong it changes that persons trust. So, I always have to make sure I keep people in mind. Can God trust you with people? Can people trust you? Are you a person that's the same everywhere you go? And finally, can you trust yourself? Can you trust in the ability or the call that God has in you to do? Do you trust in yourself? If you're untrustworthy to God, untrustworthy to people, untrustworthy to yourself then you build a lying and lazy stronghold in your life.

Listen, a lot of people are tied to a lie, tied to a facade, tied to their multiple personalities instead of being in tuned with who God wants them to be. So many people are soul tied to the idea of them but are unwilling to address their real selves. They have built this stronghold that now it's hard for them to even try to go back to being an original, it is hard for them to go back and be themselves because they are too invested in their fake life. You've got to ask yourself this question, what is the credit score of your character like Eric Thomas said? What is the value of your name? What are you known for? Out there, do people trust you? Because when you have good credit people can trust you with more, when you have bad credit people can't trust you with things or will make you pay more in interest before they commit long term. What is the value of your name? When people hear your name is it valuable, or has your actions devalued your name to them? When people hear your name would they think trust, would they think confidence? Or would they think scheme, would they think incapable, would they think negligence? What are you known for? What is your name out there in other people's conversations? Are they talking greatly about you, or poorly about you? It doesn't matter if people talk bad about you but let them talk bad because they are jealous of you, let them not talk bad because you have given them validation to do so because of your negligence.

What is your Names credit score?	Very Poor	Poor	Fair	Good	Excellent
What would you like to be known for?					
What are you practicing now that could be devaluing your name?					
What must you do to increase the value of your name?					

Social Media Rant:

Don't always put your trust in what people post because most people don't post their bad days and don't lose yourself in posting only the best side of you because you will believe you are something you are not. Social media = Fake News. Many people through insecurities try to make others believe they are happy or that they are successful when they are not. Not everyone can handle a world where likes and views determine their social value. People live for the likes, live for the views and have attached their self-worth to it to the point they will fake how they are to appease others hoping they will receive validation. People are tied to the perceptions of others. Their days are great when they receive great support and will become bad the moment they feel they are not loved.

You must love you for you and be honest with yourself and allow God to determine your value and be honest about how dope you are. I'm not saying that you air out all your grievances about yourself online, but I am saying that you should just be wise online and don't allow yourself to fall into the traps of comparisons. Don't lose yourself trying to be like someone else. I've been guilty even recently with making comparisons online and seeing preachers or people that I am quote on quote better than have more followers and likes than I do and when I see that my mind would at times go into thinking about how I can orchestrate a master plan to beat them and out shine them and I had to really pull those thoughts in and investigate my heart because that's dangerous. And instead of staying true to what God wants me to preach or move It would lead me to want to succeed off competition. Your heart is a huge place and you must search it daily because there are a lot of things that have been deposited in us through society that has us act this way. Take a break from online often and establish checkpoint times for you to check your social media. Checking your social media shouldn't take a lot of your time unless its apart of your business etc. how are you socially online? Are you too consumed?

Social Media Fast: I want you to take some time within in the next 24 hours to calculate how long you spend online daily once you have that I want you to write down the amount of minutes and hours you spend online. Be honest with yourself and write down the correct times. I want you to secondly scroll through on each social media profile for at least 2 months and write down the person you are online in comparison to you and really look to see if both people are the same. If you have spent more hours online than in your word, in prayer and working on your purpose or are living a double life you need to take a fast. If this pertains to you I want you to cut your social media time by 70% on the weekends and I want you to only spend 30 minutes on the internet (socially) each day during the week for 14 days or you can only be on the internet on the weekends for only 1 hour per day.

How many hours do you spend on social media a day?		Time →
Who are you online?	Who are you in real life?	Do these individuals match?

If you have failed the social media test pick a fast and track your progress by simply putting in the boxes below either p for pass or f failed or you can write how much time you spent online that day.						
Goals for your fast?						
What will you work on with your extra time?						
M	T	W	T	F	S	S
M	T	W	T	F	S	S
Reflection						

As I always tell people, the best way to avoid lying or cheating is to never put yourself in the position to do so. The reason why many people lose families, lose spouses, lose money is because they put themselves in positions that they are not strong enough to handle. The best way to avoid lying or cheating is to be self-controlled, and you can't be self-controlled without time with the spirit of God.

Let's talk about some **core symptoms**. The core symptoms of a person who is not trustworthy – (circle the symptoms that apply)

- they're cheaters,
- they steal,
- they're deceptive,
- pathological lying,
- they hunger for acceptance, success and attention
- they commit adultery,
- they commit emotional adultery,
- they commit spiritual adultery,
- denial, they are always denying,
- Self-deception, they deceive themselves.
- They're always secretive,
- they're hiding all the time,
- they're never open, closed individuals.
- they show you as a part of them, but that's not really them.
- boastful and fake social media profiles
- they are not people of their word
- no one trusts them
- manipulative and deceptive

If you have any of these symptoms in your life you may be struggling with being honest. Also, to avoid falling into the symptoms of these individuals you will need strong discernment from God because those who are like this can really be deceptive.

Let's talk about core solutions - **Proverbs 6:16 - 19** - *There are six things that the Lord hates, seven that are an abomination to him, haughty eyes, a lying tongue, hands that shed innocent blood, a heart that devise wicked plans, feet that make haste to run to evil, a false witness who breathes our lies and one who sows discord among brothers.* God cannot trust anyone with haughty eyes, a lying tongue, hands that shed innocent blood, a heart that devises wicked plans, feet that make haste to run to evil and a false witness and a person who sows discord among his brothers. Listen, if any one of these traits are a part of you, you are engaging with something that is an abomination to God, he cares about how you treat others, he cares about how you move around others because sometimes we forget that we are all connected. Sometimes we forget that our actions can end up hurting others; you reap what you sow. He hates the haughty eye because he knows that the eye is the window to the soul. He hates a person that has a prideful eye, a person who looks down on others and overly consider themselves. He hates a lying tongue because he knows the effects words have on others and how innocent people will put themselves in vulnerable places with those they trust. He hates hands, feet and hearts that maliciously devises plans and executes them to the point of dividing others. If you harbour any of these traits, you will never ultimately win. You are just a lonely insecure person that has no purpose. And if you are always the victim of these individuals, you must tighten up your walk with God and become more alert and sensitive to the leading of the Holy Spirit! Before I move on to the next verse notice, all these are physical traits - eyes, tongue, hands, heart, feet. Be very careful what you allow these things to do because they will hurt others and will eventually hurt you.

Proverbs 19:9 - *A false witness will not go unpunished and he who breathes out lives will perish.* Every person who is a false witness or living a false life will never go unpunished - either God will punish them eternally or their own deceit will punish them.

Proverbs 12:22 - *Lying lips are an abomination to the Lord, but those who act faithfully are in his delight.* If you want to be pleasing, be faithful; not false.

Colossians 3:9-10 - *Do not lie to one another seeing that you have put off the old self with these practices. Put on the new self which is being renewed in the knowledge after the image of his creator.* Lying is a part of the old man. You've got to always be intentional with putting away your old self; seeing that you are without excuse now that you have the spirit of God in you. People of God shouldn't lie because they know everyone deserves to hear and know the truth even if it hurts. It's best to avoid things through self-control for the future happiness and safety of others then to be selfish momentarily and then later find out your actions deeply hurt someone. If you know you are not ready to be faithful to one person don't get married, if you know you are a selfish person don't partner yourself with someone. Stay single and stay distant from individuals until you have been sanctified in that area because reckless people wreck other people's lives. Leave lying dead with your old self and let self-control through the Spirit of God guide you!

Ephesians 4:25 says *Therefore having put away falsehood let each of you speak the truth with his neighbour, for we are members one of another.* This verse lets us know that we are all connected, and a lie to another will eventually affect us.

Luke 8:17- *For nothing is hidden that will not be made manifest nor is anything secret that would not be known and come to light.* It's always best to live honestly because nothing can stay hidden before an omniscient God. God sees all, and you might as well present it to the light now before God openly puts it in the light before others.

Proverbs 12:19 - Trustful lips endure forever, but a lying tongue is but for a moment. Lying only satisfies for a moment but will soon be exposed. Listen, the truth never changes. Truthful lips endure forever, meaning if you are a truthful person then you will last a long time, you will last a long time in business, your ministry will last, your marriage will last because you're truthful. But if you have a lying tongue, what you endeavour to have for a long time will only be in your life for a few moments.

1 John 2:4 - *Whoever says I know him but does not keep his commandments is a liar and the truth is in him.* Your commitment must match your confessions. If you confess to be a friend of God, if you confess to know him then you must have commitments that match, you've got to make sure that you are a person who keeps his commandments. Many people know about God but don't truly know him. Do you really know him, or do you just know about him? Complete dedication to God, self-discipline, valuing others and valuing you will help you unite and uproot this stronghold on your life. When you build a complete dedication to God you begin to be focused on him, you will uproot this. If you allow dedication to God to build self-discipline you will begin to value others and value you, man you will love the truth of you, you would never want to be a liar, you would never want to post online a Christianity that you don't live. The truth doesn't change, and it's hard to keep up with a lie or a false life. It is best to live a truthful life than trying to keep up with three different lives. You only have one life to live, don't try to live three. And my question today is, are you truly committed? If you are committed to God, God will help you to be truthful. If you struggle in this area you really must make sure you reflect on why you lie because God can't trust a person who is not capable or willing to live truthfully.

Words				
How strong is the tie or hold in this area? →		Weak	Mild	Strong
Which areas are affected and in what way? Place a check beside each area that's affected and explain in what way in the larger box below.				
Spiritually	Mentally	Emotionally	Physically	

I want you to say this prayer if you struggle in this area –

Father I no longer want to lie anymore. I want to be the man or the woman you have for me to be. I want to be an original; not a copy. Lord, I want to live one life, not multiple. God help me to be an honest person, help me to progress forward. God help me to avoid putting myself in places that will cause me to lie. God help me not to lie to feel accepted, help me not to lie to feel enlarged. God help me to be truthful, help me to be okay with where I'm not, and help me not to lie to try to present something that I'm not. I repent of this sin now in Jesus name!

Right now, through the authority of Christ, I come against the spirit of lying and deceit and manipulation. I now see the value in myself; I now see the value in people, therefore I will no longer hurt others. I am letting go of every commitment that's going to cause me not to be who God wants me to be. Lord I am okay with where I'm at, because I know that if I'm with you I will be where you desire for me to be. Help me not to lie God, help me to live a truthful life, and help me to build the life I desire to have, and I thank you, Lord. Amen.

CHAPTER EIGHT – ADDICTIONS

An addiction is a negative attachment to a person, place, product or power.

There are two types of satisfactions that produce these types of addictions - there are eternal satisfactions, and there are temporal satisfactions.

An eternal satisfaction is a satisfaction that only Christ can give. Jesus is the only one that can truly satisfy the soul; everything else just temporarily satisfies. He is the only one that can heal the core; everything else just relieves the symptoms. God wants to redirect our hunger. Ever since we were drifted from the garden, humanity has had a negative hunger. The Bible talks about hunger, it says that they that hunger and thirst after righteousness shall be filled. The type of hunger and thirst that we should have outside of the basic needs for bodily nourishment is for our hunger and thirst to be after God's righteousness, not after things that will ruin us. The sad thing is most people go after things that only temporarily satisfies. And since Christ is the only one that can genuinely satisfy our soul we have to make sure that we continuously pursue after him. When a person neglects to pursue after the one that can eternally satisfy they will always find themselves dehydrated and malnourished.

There's something satisfying that comes with being connected to something that completely satisfies. There's a contentment that comes when you are completely satisfied and with Christ at this moment you can be completely satisfied. Now would there be wants and needs? Of course, you're human but those wants, and needs will spew out of a content spirit. So, you must ask yourself, "Am I completely satisfied? Or am I still searching for satisfaction?" Because anything that you search for outside of Jesus will only temporarily satisfy you.

It's so sad that most people are caught up in solving or removing the symptoms but never treating the core problem. What happens with people who have product addictions, people addictions, painful addictions, power addictions etc., those addictions will lure them to become attached to something that they always have to keep coming back to. The reason why the devil designed a system full of addictions is because he knows that the more people become addicted to things, the more they will pay for those things. So, when it comes to addiction to pornography and addiction to sex and addiction to the need for companionship, the addiction to video games, the addiction to drugs; people will begin to pour out of their hard-earned money to satisfy their addictions.

But the thing about Christ is, Christ is free. So, if people are freely given an eternal satisfaction to their depraved soul, then there would be no need for people going out there to satisfy their addictions. Unfortunately, the church has become addicted to growth, they have become addicted to success, they have become addicted to presentation and in doing so they are not tending to the sheep. That's why if you have a pastor or a leader who is more consumed with his/her brand or identity you will find their sheep not taken care of. That's why our job as individuals is to make disciples and to bring people to Christ so that Christ can ease their soul. A soul not eased is a restless soul, and most people are walking throughout life with a restless soul which continues to reach out to things that they think will eternally satisfy them.

Every addiction will leave you broke and begging. Demons know that the best way to get into a person's pocket is to cause them to be addicted. That's why they put chemicals in our foods to keep us addicted. You are addicted to those Oreo's for a reason; you're addicted to those cookies for a reason, you're addicted to that beverage for a reason. Because they know if I can get the taste buds to feel sensationalized, if I can get the taste buds to get so consumed with what they tasted then you will like I did for years leave my bed to go to 7/11 to get two honey buns. It's crazy how the bulk of our enjoyment is a small percentage. What I mean by that, the taste buds or your tongue is a small percentage of the entire digestive system. When you eat food, first you taste, then it goes into your oesophagus, then it goes into your stomach, then it goes into the small and large intestines, then it's out the back end. But what people fail to realize is when you focus on the small percentage versus the entire process you will find yourself sick. Most people are sick today because they're more consumed with how things taste versus how things transition throughout their body. We got to make sure we focus on the transitional process, not just the tasting process.

That's why the Bible talks about not awakening love before it's time, do not touch things before it's time, do not engage in things before your time of maturity because the enemy knows if I can get you to taste and see that it feels good or seems good, then you'll think it's good. And you will trade the greatness and the necessity of the Christ for something engineered or constructed in a laboratory. That's why we've got to get to a place where we say, "God, I want my hunger and thirst to be behind the trail of righteousness. Because if I hunger and thirst after righteousness I truly will be filled." But when you chase after these things, these people and the vengeance of your painful experiences, and for power then you'll always find yourself empty. Jesus is the only one that can truly satisfy your soul.

The layers of an addiction,

There are four layers - there are physical/biological, emotional, mental, and spiritual. Let's break each one down.

The goal is to cause your spirit man to be anorexic or neglected. They understand that we are spiritual beings in an earthly existence. It's crazy that the bulk of mankind focuses on the external, the outside versus the spiritual. They understand the best way to get a person addicted is to cause their spirit man to be darkened. My question to you is, how often do you spend time with God? I say you should feed off the Word of God as often as you feed your body. If you feed your body or your emotions and your mind as far as entertainment more so than your spirit man, then you will have a lopsided earthly experience.

Lopsided experiences are birthed when both areas or one area is neglected, and the other area is overly fed. The best balance is when the spirit man is fed more so than the rest. If I can cause a spirit man of an individual to be darkened, neglected, anorexic, then I will now have access to the other compartments (soul and body). They understand that when a person goes through different experiences and they begin to fall into the jaws of influences then they will have experiences that will cause mental and emotional strain. Mental and emotional strain is when these areas have been neglected and have not been protected. Whenever there is a strain on the soul realm stress is inevitable. Satan wants to stress your mind, your emotions, and your soul and if he knows that Christ is the only one that can ease these things he will do whatever it takes to keep you from him. If he can keep you from Jesus then your spirit man will not be submitted enough to be led by the holy spirit and you will be susceptible to influences that will lead you to being addicted mentally, emotionally and physically.

There are two-folds to this - they want you to have a curiosity for experiences and to experience pain from experiences. They understand if I can get you to have a painful experience or to have you curious about certain experiences then I could cause you to be so focused on what has happened to you or what you would like to happen that it will cause you to be set up for a **trap**. Because they know for a fact there's nothing more painful than a fresh experience that went bad. And when a person feels that fresh pain there will be certain types of emotions that will build - hate, resentment, envy, jealousy, pride, super-sized ambitions will begin to boil, and now the emotions that were supposed to be led by the Spirit is now led by vengeance, aspirations, jealousy, and pride. Now this person is on this fixated prowl to try and vindicate their identity or if a person is curious of experiences, then that person will be latched on to thought of "I just want to try it."

That's why you have a lot of young people trying sex, trying drugs because of the allure, the curiosity that builds from the false enjoyment of it. Because what's marketed throughout the world is false enjoyments. They only show you the heightened experiences of something but never show you the hell that follows. So when a spirit man is darkened and there's a strain or stress on the mind, the need for, which should be for Christ, is now for a product or a person leading to a cycle of pain.

Now when the mind and the emotions are pressured to taste something or to engage with something, the devil understands just how sensitive the biology of a person's body is. When you give a child water, and then you give a child Kool-Aid, the heightened taste of the sugar causes the child to desperately want the Kool-Aid more than the water, the soda more than water, the cupcakes more than carrots. So now you have reversed engineered the taste experience. If you can reverse engineer, the taste experience and cause people to have a desired taste for something then you now have access to their purpose and access to their life. Now if you can cause a person to be biologically or physically addicted to sex, you will have a higher chance of giving them an STD. If you can have a person to have a biological addiction to anything edible, you can now put chemicals in there foods to destroy their bodies. The devil is after your purpose because the longer you exist with a heart burning with purpose, the higher the chance you have of destroying his kingdom.

How do we break the layers of addictions?

First, as I always say you have to break it in the spirit realm. We are spirit beings and our power is best exercised in the spirit realm. Whatever happens in the spirit realm then floods into the natural. It's crazy how we go to the natural first then the spiritual second or if at all. We're supposed to go to the spirit realm first and stay on that thing until it manifests in the natural world - meaning if you have an addiction to pornography you've got to break the allegiance you have created subconscious or consciously with the enemy, you have to say, "Through the blood of Jesus and through what He has done for me I sever my allegiance, or tie to pornography, to lust." You have to get to the core and say, "I forgive my dad who did this or I forgive my mom who did this, who opened the door for my addiction." You have to go all the way back to when it was conceived and break your allegiance in the spirit realm through the blood of Jesus.

Once it has been broken in the spirit realm you now have to set support systems and welcome Godly accountability. But before it's even broken in the spirit realm, you've got to submit and be committed. The Bible says submit yourself to God, resist devil, and he will flee." You can't resist the devil and expect him to flee if you are not fully submitted to God. You've got to be fully submitted and fully persuaded, because when you are you will now have the authority and the passion to break its hold.

Support Systems

Support systems are systems designed to support something while it's being rebuilt or being built. Before you start building you've got to demolish something. You have to make sure that your old man has been demolished and the debris has been cleared for you to build your new man. But while this new building, your new self is being built you got to make sure you have support systems in place to guard the walls and to hold up what's being built so that as it's being built your new life will be guarded into maturity. We need support systems to support us during this new journey and we need to go to great lengths to ensure we are built securely, meaning I'm going to make sure I have no Wi-Fi in my house for however long. I'm going to make sure I remove anything and everything that will help me sin. Like I always say never have sin within arm's reach because during moments of vulnerability if its close you will reach for it. I've got to always make sure that my old sin is not easily accessible because when you're fresh out of being in sin with something your body and soul are still connected to the memories and habits of it.

In order for there to be deep healing there needs to be deep confession and in order for there to be deep confession there needs to be deep community and deep fellowship with Christ. If we really take the time to slow our lives down and self-examine our hearts, we would be able to track where we need healing. Who you are and what you're doing right now stems from either a hurt place or a healed place. No one left alone with a wound will receive healing. It's impossible to overcome a drug, porn, or person addiction by yourself. But the real question is how bad do you want to be healed?

The enemy wants you to be silent about your sins, because if you're silent about your sins and you never confess them amongst a group of people who can be trusted, then you will never overcome. You've got to have a place where you and your new life can be safe. Next you've got to fast, you've got to read, you've got to pray, you've got to get plugged in, you've got to be productive, not busy. What I mean by that is you've got to start being proactive in the process. You have to be intentional and establish a why. Why do you want to be free? Is what I'm doing really benefiting me? It's pointless to be addicted to something that cannot save.

Your level of freedom is predicated on how free you really are. Those who are in Christ are immediately free from the penalty of hell but may not immediately be free from physical, emotional or mental addictions. They have the power to walk in freedom in each area but there requires a certain level of cooperation and closeness to God to be completely free. Right now if you are bearing fruit from true conversion, then your spirit is free but the real question is where are you still bound mentally, physically or emotionally? Once you realize that there is so much in stored for you both tangibly and intangibly then you will really seek to find freedom in all areas of your life. You would seek to forgive, to be productive in your purpose, to love everyone because you know one day you are going to be held accountable for what you did in your body and you don't want God to show you how people were affected by you being bound. Free people free people.

Moderation

Indulgence is the enemy of moderation. Addictions occur when things are not used in moderation or are used improperly. Not everything under the firmament was created by God. Some things were engineered by individuals to hurt us. God wants us to use what was created for us specifically in moderation and with the right motives. Using things in moderation but with the wrong motives is sin. God cares about how we interact and use things. Anything used outside of its proper use or out of moderation will hurt you. There is nothing wrong with eating, watching entertainment, or having extracurricular activities but when those things are used to try and heal an emotional wound or to overcome a mental barrier you are in danger of forming an addiction. The devil wants you to go anywhere but to God for your emotional or mental well-being. Nothing can satisfy your soul like God. Every addiction a person has can be traced back to a moment of hurt or neglect. What are you addicted too? What could have possibly formed your addiction?

Let's look at some scriptures. 2 Corinthians 12:9 says - *But he said to me, my grace is sufficient for you, for my power is made perfect in weakness. Therefore I will boast all the more gladly of my weaknesses so that the power of Christ may rest upon me.*

Pride reveals weakness humility reveals wisdom. A lot of people are operating on their own sufficiency through pride instead of embracing God's sufficiency. We have limits God doesn't. Every day we experience weakness, and we experience our limits. It's in those moments we need to be humble and know that God is the only one that can truly sustain us. The sad thing is many people instead of going to God when they experience weakness they go to everything and everyone else. There is nothing on the planet that can sustain us like God. He is the only one with the grace, patience and understanding to help navigate us through any situation. Before we can act strongly we must first acknowledge that we are weak. A person that refuses to acknowledge they are weak is a person who is truly weak. Pride and hostility towards God keep many people from one acknowledging that they are weak two asking for divine help and three boasting in our weakness. In order to truly be successful we have to be humble enough to ask for help and not just ask for help but to also wait and embrace the power that comes when we acknowledge and ask. The more we do this and see and feel the supernatural support from God we will boast more in his ability than in our abilities.

We will boast the more gladly every time that we are incapable of our own strength because it will give us the opportunity to witness a miracle. But if you never acknowledge or ask, you will never feel the support and if you never feel the support, you will try and fill that void with something else other than God. I remember times in my early to mid-twenties when I was going through a very stressful time in my life I would at moments when I was really stressed go and try and sustain myself through pornography. I would look online to see how pornography and masturbation would eliminate stress and instead of going to God I would practice this sin to feel "stress free" but what I didn't realize was this sin was only deepening itself in me and even though it felt like it was doing its job I found myself watching for more than just stress relief. That addiction did nothing for me but altered my expectations of women and formulate unrealistic standards of them as well. But God through his mercy renewed my mind and now when I feel stressed I acknowledge to God that I am weak, I ask for his support and I embrace my support systems. It was not easy but it was definitely worth it, and God can do the same for you but you must know that you and your habits are incapable alone of sustaining you and you need his power to overcome any addiction. I see this too when I preach. I work at a title one school here in Charlotte and my responsibilities support the top behavioural students in our school; which means many of my days are full of dealing with dire situations and insubordinate students. When Thursday's come, I not only work but also have to speak at night. There be times when I am dog tired and don't feel like preaching not that I don't care about the people I just don't have the energy but when I look to heaven and tell God man I'm weak he always comes through. I may be tired when I get there and I may be tired 3 minutes before its time to preach but when I sit on that chair a supernatural energy comes over me and through his power I execute at a high level. I don't need no coffee, I don't need no drugs all I need is him and I get excited when he tells me to do something and I'm weak because I know he is going to operate strongly through me.

1 John 3:8 says - *Whoever makes a practice of sinning is of the devil, for the devil has been sinning from the beginning.*

Who are you of? The proof is in your actions. You are only going to perform based on the power you choose to operate out of. Many people are working for the devil and don't even know it. They are allowing his system to fuel them with perspectives on lifestyle choices causing them to function through those perspectives. We practice the perspectives we hold. You will become what you think and you will navigate through life as an image of the thoughts you think. The devil's main objective is for you and me to bear his image the image of rebellion. All sins are forms of rebellion - rebelling from the original image of God. When we take our eyes off God we begin to allow sinful perspectives to form in our minds and when we allow these perspectives to form in our minds we begin to practice them. We begin to practice our perspectives on sexuality, sex, giving, worship etc. you can't expect to perform well for God if you are practicing sin. Practice leads to perfection. You will perfect what you practice it's sad that many of us practice more sin than we do the things of God. God wants you to think like him. He wants you to be set apart so that he can use you to put to end the work of Satan not practice them. Be very careful what you repeat because what you repeat will be your rituals and your rituals will either reward you or ruin you. What are you repeating?

1 Corinthians 6:12 - *All things are lawful for me, but not all things are helpful.*

Just because it is lawful does not mean it is helpful. There are many lawful things in our country, or in your country if you are not in the United States, that are a lawful, but are not helpful. They are lawful for your body to do, but they are not helpful for the spirit of God working through you. Sex outside of marriage is lawful, perverted relationships are lawful, drinking and some drugs are lawful, overeating is lawful; but it is not helpful. I want you right now to write down things that are lawful but not helpful. When you understand that you will begin to say, "Hey, is what I am doing helpful even though it's lawful?" Just because there's a clearance in the devil's world to do it doesn't mean that you should engage with it. Many lawful things turn into addictions.

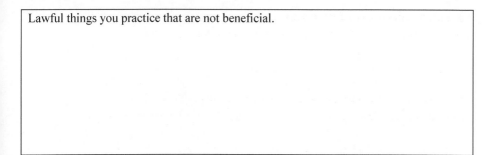

Lawful things you practice that are not beneficial.

Ephesians 5:18 - *And do not get drunk with wine the for that is debauchery. But be filled with the spirit.*

What are you full of? It is best to be full of the spirit than to be full or high off any substance. Why be high off an earthly substance when I am connected to the most high? You have access to peace through the Most High; you don't have to get high to be at peace. You can go to God right now and have peace. Even in the midst of misunderstandings, confusions he says I'll give you a peace that surpasses understanding. Since we don't understand what we are going through at times we go to drugs or other forms of ecstasy to get a taste of "peace" but that peace only last as long as its high and once you come down you are still left with the same problems you tried to float away from. But when you are filled with the spirit you don't have to seek a high because you are connected to him and his high will lead you to see the highest point of all of your situations he will show you how to address your situations not avoid them and he will show you the highest perspectives on manhood, womanhood etc.

Proverbs 11:17 - *A man who is kind benefits himself, but a cruel man hurts himself.*

Kindness is a part of the fruit of the spirit and it is essential for caring for yourself and for others. Kind is not blind meaning true kindness sees deeper than what most people see. A kind person endeavours to see the well-being of others and in return will receive well-being. This proverb lets us know the fruit of being kind and cruel. A kind person will in return reap kindness and gentleness because their countenance and their character are genuine and people with a kind heart always receive kindness in return but when a person is cruel they usually end up alone. Right now I am rich not because of how much money I have but because of how many rich relationships I have. If I were to lose my job today, I know I would be takin care of because of the relationships I have built. Who is going to cross a

171

bridge to help you if you burned them all? That's why it's important to treat everyone kind because in the end you will help yourself. How many bridges have you burned?

Cruelty is a reflection of self-hate, and wherever there is self-hate, there are addictions. It's hard to love others when you don't love yourself. Many people are addicted today because they don't love themselves or deep down inside they are trying to run away from a problem. Anything used in excess is dangerous. Even drinking too much water at one time can kill you. What are you doing in excess and what are you doing beyond its normal limits because whatever that is I'm sure you can trace it to a place of hurt or insecurity. Today rewind and look into your heart and see what is keeping you from being kind to yourself and towards others.

What are you doing in excess now that could hurt you in the future?

Nothing in this life can heal you from an addiction other than God. To overcome an addiction requires the transference of desire and only the divine can do that. The bible says that it is the goodness of God that draws man back into repentance. Once we have tasted the goodness of God, we will at that moment feel the difference between who God is and what we crave. The woman at the well knew this all too well. This woman was a prostitute she was considered one of if not the lease in her community. You can tell she was by the time she went to the well to draw her water. Most women during that time either went early in the morning or late in the evening when it was cool. The outsiders though went during the noon of the day to avoid the looks and the stares from the privileged. But Jesus being intentional that he was sat at the well to wait for her not when it was cool but when the day was its hottest and was kind enough to endure the heat to have a life-changing conversation with her. He began to paint the picture of the differences between natural thirst and spiritual thirst and by the time he finished the final stroke on the canvas of her mind her life was changed. Jesus will always meet you at your previous place of satisfaction and let you know that if your soul drinks of him you will never thirst again. Her heart rested in the arms of her lovers she even had multiple husbands, and the one she was with wasn't hers. By hearing her story, we can see her insecurities or the cruelty she was putting herself through but when He showed her gently her heart and utilized her forefathers well, as an illustration, she impacted her community. The same person that was shunned by her community was the person God used to save her community. Who the Son sets free is free indeed. It's not always those who preach the gospel that saves people it's those that have been radically changed by the gospel that does. Grace + Truth = Salvation. Why keep going back to your well over and over again. Every addiction requires you to come back to it but with Jesus you truly only have to come once. Once she met him she was never the same. Once you meet the real Jesus you will no longer desire old addictions and if you ever fall back into them you will be disgusted!

Addictions						
How strong is the tie or hold in this area? →				Weak	Mild	Strong
Which areas are affected and in what way? Place a check beside each area that's affected and explain in what way in the larger box below.						
Spiritually		Mentally		Emotionally		Physically

Let's break these addictions in the sprit realm now let's start with the prayer below.

Heavenly Father, I thank you for being such a caring father and for pursuing me despite my addictions. I repent now Father for allowing (list below whatever conceived your addictions)

_____

_____

to create such a void in my life causing me to become addicted. I repent for being addicted to the following people

_____

_____

To the following places

_____

_____

And to the following products

_____

_____

I cancel my improper allegiance to these people and things now in Jesus Name!

Satan through the authority of Jesus I break my connection to you in this area and I cancel every plot and scheme from this day forward. You no longer have any legal rights into my life and I severe these addictions and your place in my life now in Jesus name!

Holy Spirit lead me, guide me, enrich me, support me, and sustain me. Give me a new hunger, give me a new thirst after more righteousness and help me to put an end to every demonic work in my life mentally, emotionally and physically. I appreciate you for all you do! Amen!

My Support Systems

What were you addicted to →	Mentally	Emotionally	Physically
How were they conceived? →			

What areas in your life are not submitted to God that could cause these addictions to come back again?

What support systems do you need to help you stay free in each area?

CHAPTER NINE – SEXUAL PURITY

The core of people's desire for sex is lust. Lust is an overbearing desire for something. When a person desires something beyond their level of maturity and outside the lines God has set, then they are setting themselves up to fail. God wants us to have self-control and to be able to manage our urges. Urges comes from the word urgency. The enemy wants us to be led by our urges. Whenever we feel urges, we need to ask ourselves what umbrella of influence am I under; am I in an environment that is drawing at these urges out or am I experiencing the effects of drifting from God? Lust can't be managed; it must be diluted and destroyed. Lust cannot be trusted. People say love is blind, but love is not blind, infatuation is. Lust will blindly take you places you never intended to go. It will take you from desiring sexual pleasure individually to desiring sexual pleasure from the opposite sex to desiring sexual pleasures from a minor or from the same sex. Lust has no boundaries, and its agenda is after your purity of mind.

Sex is one of the most powerful experiences on the planet it is so powerful that it was only reserved for marriage. Anything used outside of its proper place will cause immediate harm. Every person that engages with sexual activity outside of marriage suffers immediate harm even if it's not immediately noticed. Sexual activity damages us when it is not used properly. God invented sex and the inventor is the best one to explain its best use. So many people are damaging themselves and their future relationships and don't even know it. Sex is good but sex becomes bad when it is used outside of a marriage that is submitted to God.

Sensuality is what fuels the carnal need for sex. Sensuality by definition is the carnal enjoyment, expression or pursuit of sexual pleasure. Sensuality is what perverts sex. There is nothing wrong with the enjoyment, expression or pursuit of sexual pleasure in the context of marriage but when a person is pursuing these sexual pleasures for the sole purpose to fulfil their selfish sexual desires then they are in sin even in marriage. Sex within marriage was designed to be a selfless expression of love not a selfish one. Sex should be expressed in a marriage where mutual selfless love exists.

There's a cause to every effect.

We all came here though the sexual intercourse of a man and a woman though many of us may not know the backstory of that moment we all are aware of how powerful sex is. That one moment can cause the amazing process of developing a human being. But sex just doesn't begin with intercourse it begins with a series of events, emotions, and entrapments. This system aims to fuel our carnal desires. Its goal is to have us be consumed with our urges. Nothing just happens everything was caused. I'm pretty sure you can trace all the way back to the moment you knew you was headed in the wrong direction sexually. I am sure you will notice as you take that trip down through memory lane all of the events and emotions that led to you engaging into that sexual activity. I am also sure you would notice all the exists God had lined up for you to take to avoid the snares of the temptation, but you ignored it. We all have been guilty whether it was sexual or any other carnal/ sinful behaviour but we must understand that nothing just happens. Urges are being brought to the surface for a reason because the enemy knows that whenever a person is being led more by their urges than by godly discernment, they will always fall into sin. This system uses fashion, pornography and other resources to make it extremely difficult for anyone not to be affected by it. Its effects leads us to want to express how we feel. Many people try to solve the effects of their sensuality but are unaware of how to deal with the causes.

The need for love

True love is hard to find but it is present everywhere. God is love but a carnal heart will ignore or avoid the obvious to pursue what it thinks is true love. That's why the Bible says no one seeks for God and in another place it says that He is the one that pursues because he knows that left alone without revelation from himself we will never seek him. We have to see to seek and if our perception is perverted, we will never be able to see God the way he desires to be seen. This system is designed for us to fall into the counterfeits of love instead of walking in true love. Many of our experiences were birthed out of our need for love especially through our low self-esteem. Many people right now do not love themselves or if they do they don't like themselves. Sexual activity was never to be something you settle for. It was designed to be enjoyed by two friends one male and one woman under the umbrella of marriage. When our esteem is low we set ourselves up to be hurt. As I said before once we disconnect ourselves from God, we depreciate. Whatever area in your life right now that is not connected fully to God has depreciated in value. Satan wants us to feel low because if we feel low we will do lowly things.

All of us desire love, but how many of us actually love ourselves. Someone who is in love with God and love himself or herself accurately will never settle for anything that possesses a threat to their relationship with God, their purpose, their finances or to their loved ones. People who truly value themselves protect themselves. Those who know who they are to God and to those around them will run away from anything that will cause them to depreciate in value. Sex outside of marriage is the fruit of low self-esteem and the lack of self-control. Without these two at a high level you will find yourself in compromising situations. How do you see you? Do you love you or does your lack of love for yourself have you in the arms or the bedroom of someone who too has low self-esteem and who lacks self-control?

What do you love about yourself?	What do you not love about yourself?

What is left vulnerable in your life due to you not loving yourself?

What is the root cause to your low self-esteem?

179

Counterfeit pleasures

Sexual activity feels great in the moment but moments later will always have you feeling empty. Demons do not want you to taste how it feels to be content in God. God is like a cold glass of water after a long day's work in the sun. He is like a nice breeze after a long summer. He is refreshment to the soul. True natural pleasure comes from obedience to God. Sexual activity from lust cannot compare to sexual activity from love shared with your best friend in marriage. Satan's system is designed to ensure we NEVER feel what it feels like to be completely satisfied by God. He doesn't want us to feel the quality of pleasure when things are done the right way. God's truth about the main points of the human existence is in his word. He is not trying to keep you from fun he just wants us to have fun safely. His fences are not there to keep you from having fun but to protect you from the consequences of sin. No one who does anything outside of the will of God is deeply satisfied.

False enjoyments will always lead to selfish expressions. Selfish expressions will always lead to carnal pursuits. When people are "enjoying" the world they are trapped in a warped emotional experience we know as ecstasy. Ecstasy is a brief moment of satisfaction designed to build an emotional addiction. Right now, your mind and body can remember every registered, "great" sexual experience of yours. Sometimes during moments of weakness, it gives you the chills. Those chills are designed to lure you to express that experience again hoping to feel what you once felt or to see what feelings are beyond it. These false enjoyments are the enjoyments that are keeping millions of people from walking faithfully with God. It's hard for a baby Christian to follow God wholeheartedly if they are still struggling with soul ties to a sexual experience. Every addiction when being weaned off has withdrawals. The withdrawal period is a nightmare to people and Satan loves it. He wants you and me to fail repeatedly during the withdrawal period because he knows that the withdrawal period from a sexual addiction can break the will of any person. Every addiction was designed to have this as a buffer pulling people back into the addiction. That's why we were told not to awaken love before the time because love expressed sexually is dangerous to anyone not mature enough to handle it. People may be skilled at sex, but they are still inwardly bruised. Love was meant to be awaken within the confines of marriage because it will literally destroy anyone outside of it. Why do you want to express your love is the question you should ask yourself before you go over his house or set the vibe before she comes over. If you can sin beyond your truthful answer then you may not be truly saved. If we are truly honest with ourselves, we would talk ourselves right out of sexual sin or if we do fall due to not having the right support systems then once it is done you will be highly disgusted.

Your body was not meant to be triggered in a certain way immaturely because once triggered it will begin to register feelings, emotions, and memories all registering this person as the sole person for your sexual pleasure. The crazy thing is these sensors go haywire when there are multiple people being registered. Its like driving a car with 5 people in the front passenger seat. Its hard for anyone to try and operate a normal life with all those sexual experiences in them. How many people are you still carrying? Sexual sin is overrated and it under delivers. Satan knows the game and knows how to play it with us individually. His demons were assigned to create and fuel a hypersexual culture that advertises immediate enjoyment without the dangers it brings; his slogan is like Nike Just Do It but does not say what it will do to you. He wants you to experience it immediately knowing that it will have you hooked for life. Like I said before enslaved people make money for industries not freed people. If I get you addicted to sex at 15 or to pornography at 14, then I can have you for LIFE! If I can get you full of low self-esteem and have you meet a person with a lack of self-control, then I can have you addicted potentially for life. If I can get you to have sex just one more time at 21, I just might be able to get you pregnant and have you struggle for 12 years. He loves babies having babies because these babes are still trying to find themselves and how can you help someone find themselves if you are still trying to find you. He wants your earthly life because your eternal one is of no value to him. Who owned the bulk of your life to this point? Answer honestly.

False enjoyments lead to false expectations. And one of the false enjoyments that does this is pornography. For those who have been following me for some time heard about my struggle with pornography. It began for me in a basement many years ago with channel 95. You know the channels that wasn't available on regular cable but if you hold the antenna just right you can get a somewhat clear picture… well that's when it began. My first interactions with it wasn't enjoyable because I felt deeply saddened by my sins because growing up I really loved God and I thought I was going to hell if I did it but it was when I got older that I began to get back into it when I was in college with faster internet. See back in my day (I'm saying it like I'm super old) we had dial-up so my traps were pictures but it took like 45 minutes for a full picture to show so it was pointless but when I got to college and I had my own dorm room with high-speed internet I was then introduced to pornography at a higher level, and I was addicted due to college being such a stressful time for me. I would make excuses about it saying that it was ok to do seeing that there were physical and emotional health benefits but what I became aware over time was that not everything that offers physical or emotional benefits truly benefits your soul.

Besides all that, the main problem was the false expectations it was building in me and within those who were around me. People would come to me for advice and I would notice in their words that the real reason they are not in love with their spouse was because they were still in lust. I even noticed it in my early relationships how everything I did was designed to manipulate a girl to satisfy my sexual desires I would do anything to ensure I got off by the end of the night and when I realised that was witchcraft I was brought to deep repentance. Sins done subtlety always have deeper meaning to them; what we think is ok God screams; not ok. We must always think deeper and see the sin for what it really is. Pornography will lead you down a path of treating women like bananas peel them, use them and discard the wrapper - the same for women with sex toys the need for constant pleasure during "drawn out" seasons of waiting on God leads to midnight pleasures. On-demand love leads to damaged love. It damages the hearts of those that love us. See a man's penis is not on demand like a toy and it doesn't vibrate as such. Those mechanically inspired vibrations will register unrealistic expectations and pleasures that maybe your soon to be husband can't match. We all must look at our nightly sins and really think is it worth it. Selfless love is the best kind of love. We each were created to be people that pleased not products of pleasure. Nobody can compete with the false expectations of pornography, and sex toys. Like I tell every man and woman those individuals in the porn videos are professionals meaning not everyone can do the moves they can do or are built the way they are. Remember it's a film with makeup and blemishes, for the most part, covered up and the individuals had surgery to make themselves the sizes they are. Most women and men cannot fulfil the expectations in these porn's and if not careful it will warp your mind and have you extremely disappointed with the love of your life. Many people are not looking for the love of their lives but the lust of their lives they want on demand sexual satisfaction but forget that the other person who is a non-professional is a person with their own needs and standards. Many of us our minds have been outworked sexually and we wonder why we are always frustrated in our relationships. The greatest form of soul-tie is formed out of sexual activity because unlike other sins sexual sin hurts us more than it does the other person. Many people are walking around today still tied to a sexual moment done years ago and tied to people from years ago. We were only meant to be with one person (unless after divorce or the death of a spouse). When we add multiple people sexually into our lives it leaves us mentally, emotionally and even physically damaged.

How many sexual partners have you had? →	#
List them below and beside their names write pleasurable or non-pleasurable	

How are these past or current sexual experiences affecting you now and how could they affect you in the future?

Why do you want to express yourself sexually and is it truly worth it?

When your sexual addiction conceived and what is feeding it?

Describe your withdrawal symptoms and write down what support systems can help draw you out of it. (The Prayer will be listed at the end)

How sexual baggage destroys families.

Marriage is a holy union God designed to build a connection so strong that it will affect generations to come. Imagine where our world would be today if families were submitted to God and love was patient, kind and genuine. Imagine where we would be today if marriage was held to a high honour. The bulk of marriages are filled with people who preyed for love instead of prayed to be ready for love. So many people are bringing in so much baggage into their marriages expecting the other person to unpack them instead of allowing God to unpack them prior. There are so many layers to us, and many of us have only scratch the surface of what it means to be depraved. The bible says that our hearts are so desperately wicked to the point that we need desperate help. It's crazy how many people really think they are ok. No one is ok until they are glorified in the presence of God. This should put us in a constant state of humility because at any moment something from the basement of our hearts will rise and manifest itself out of our mouth or hands. God cares about how clean every floor of your heart is. Are you truly willing to see your heart for what it really is? Marriage is a gift from God it's a union designed to be a resource by which God can show his glory to the world. He wants the world to see how two different people with two different backgrounds can come together supernaturally and though not perfect do something amazing and build a legacy that affected the world. The best way to ruin this is through insecurities and sexual sins. Satan wants to pervert marriage and he does it through infusing it with undealt with issues. How many tabs do you have still open on the screen of your heart? How many modules are 30% completed. No serious company hires someone with unfinished paperwork so why do we allow people into our lives with undealt with issues.

Now let me make this clear wholeness does not mean perfect. Wholeness means **ready**. It means **able**. When a man and woman come together, they are not going to be perfect but they are going to be prepared and progressive in their selflessness to the point that they inspire you daily in their love for you. But it's hard to be this individual if you are still being held up by your past or still struggling with a hidden sexual sin. When these memories or actions are present in a marriage, it stifles its growth. It becomes a cancer. The need for love doesn't qualify you as ready for love. So many people are currently soul tied to past sexual encounters that it becomes an unnecessary burden to the one joined to them. If you are single now wait because it's better to wait years for the one then to waste years with the wrong one. Sexual sins affect you long past the sexual act and it affects those you marry. Lust is for the moment love is for the moments. A person can't truly love you if they are full of lust because there will always be a conflict of interest. That spirit of lust will always aim to consume the energy of the other. Demons run off our negative energy. They utilize hurt people to hurt others just to get their full for the day. They love the effect adultery has on a man or a woman they love the residue effects rape and molestation has on people they love what cheating does because they know those acts will cause deep wounds in a person's heart and could affect them for years. At the core of everything is energy. Your energy will determine your execution. Energy = vibrations. You heard the phrase don't kill my vibe? Vibes are real. A person with a negative vibe can be felt the moment you even hear they are coming. That is whys it's important to marry someone with positive energy because being yoked up with a person with a lustful, prideful, selfish vibe will immediately or inevitably affect you.

That's why it's important for you to define your vibe and to make sure you catch a divine vibe before you walk out your house every day because if you don't this controlled demonic system will try to turn you into a negative vibe. Lust is a vibration it sends off signals way before potential intercourse happens. It lurks to find individuals who have been lured away from God. The safest place is in the presence of God other places will try to lure you into deep demonic traps designed to cause you to sink far below your worth and become soul tied to an individual through sex or through the scripture that says that it is better to marry than to burn with passion which then leads you to being married to a person with so much baggage. Marriage is a magnifying glass it reveals the heart. Everything feels great within lustful moments but when the sex settles, and the lust demon has been satisfied you are left with a person you don't even love. Selfless love is the key. If you don't truly love yourself how will you know how to be loved and if you are not in love with the one who is love you surely wont know how to be loved. Love is a person, and he is the only one that can show you how to love but you have to be patient. God is the doctor his people are the nurses; you must allow him to heal you privately before its times to join you into a marriage. So many people spend their entire singleness wanting a relationship but do not spend that time working to be prepared. People think that all they must have is a degree or some wit and they are set; NO, it takes patience and understanding, selflessness and divine love to sustain a marriage and not being whole from your past sexual experiences will affect the person you desire to be with. You cannot expect your marriage or your future one to be pure if you are sexually impure because what you practice will be pushed through to your children and then into your children's children and now you will have to deal with your sinful fruits being manifested in your children. Do you care about your legacy because if you do you will keep your legs closed.

What baggage is in your heart?	How could they affect your current or future relationship?

Before you enter a marriage, you must be set free from the soul ties and strongholds in your life. So many people are stuck in pornography and don't know how to get out; stuck in sexual appetites and can't get the taste out of their mouths. The only way to be free is through Christ, a solid Christian community and your calling. Christ will help set you free and will then surround you with people with formula's of freedom and then will show you your purpose to focus on. What keeps me safe from sexual sin is seeing the sin for what it really is. Me being a virgin today reflects seeing sex for what it could do. My mom shared with me the power of sex and that one wrong move can lead to the delay of my purpose. That's why it's important to know your purpose early because you will know what to partake of and what not to partake of. When your value is in God and in your purpose you will avoid anything and anyone that possess a threat to it and you will seek to see your purpose through to the end. Sexual strongholds are real, and they are used to hold your purity and your marriage back. Love is for the moments and love cares about all moments of marriage. A man addicted to porn only cares about sexual moments but a man in love with his wife and with God cares about the needs of his wife above his own. Self-control as a trait in your significant other is important because wherever they lack self-control will try to control you.

Where do you lack self-control?

What is your purpose and how can sexual sin affect it?

God's perfect timing.

God knows exactly what you like and knows exactly what you need. He is not going to give you someone who you are not sexually attracted to. Sexual attraction is important but that attraction can be manifested in lustful action. Sex is not bad it is good; it was designed to deepen the love of two people and to bear children. God knows your type more than you do that's why he delays things so that your real type can be seen. See the type of woman I wanted at 21 is not the same woman I realized was suited for me at 32. Maturity leads to clear sight. The wiser you become the more you will begin to see what you really like in a person. But sexual activity outside of marriage clouds that judgement. How can you judge a righteous judgement if you are practicing unrighteousness? You have to be in right standing to see rightly. I say all this to say that God is not some random mate picker and just sends you someone and says I guess this one will do but he knows how important sex is in a marriage he knows how it deepens love but we have to make sure we match what we like.

Self-love is a progressive form of love. It endeavours to morph and mature into a better version each day. A day not used for growth is a day wasted. Every day you should be practicing something new to increase the attraction. Subtraction and stagnation dilutes attraction. Never take away from what drew the person to you in the first place because that will lead to frustration. Always build on your best features or in other words don't let yourself go. Don't make it hard for your wife or husband to be faithful because you wane in your attraction. When you love yourself you add to who you are if you don't love yourself you will take away from who you are. Get in that gym, change your diet, find your purpose and spend everyday focused on growth. See lust subtracts love adds; lust divides love multiples. There is nothing worse than being in a relationship with a person that subtracts and divides all your time and never adds to you or multiplies you. What can you teach them? A person full of selfless love is only concerned about serving you period. Thays why it's important for both parties to be completely submitted to God so that if things are getting tough and out of line you know that when God deals with them they will change. Kanye and Jay z said what's a God to a non-believer and that's true if they won't listen to God what makes you think they will listen to you. God has a perfect timing for you to awaken love. But do you know what's even more important than the timing of promotion the season of preparation that precedes it. You have the free will to settle you have the free will to seek, conquer and marry but don't come running to God for help when it doesn't work.

God's way is always the best way and he graces us with seasons to prepare so that when it is time you will fully be able to function. A good company always ensures that their new hires are fully equipped to do their job - they do this so that the new hire cannot say they weren't trained properly. God does the same; he will never promote you to a place he does not feel confident that you are equipped to handle. You can't just be equipped you have to know how to use the equipment. God is not going to equip you with a helpmate if you are not going to treat her right or vice versa. He is only going to join what he knows is whole. Why go out and try to test drive to see what you like when you can just let God custom make you a spouse. You are not smart enough to "build a boo" you have to let God build them. God knows what the perfect size is for you God knows how tall you like him or her. He knows how to match values and standards and even if they don't match perfectly which rarely happens they will at least be selfless enough to grow and learn. He knows the level of patience and grace they will need to deal with you because we all aren't equal in grace, mercy, and patience and that's ok. Certain people are made for each other because they have been dealt a level of grace to empathize, understand and grow with you. God knows it all and you don't have to sexually test drive to see if she or he can sustain you sexually God has that covered. Let him take care of all of that because lustful sex cannot compare to sex made out of love. Aren't you tired of having sex with people whose hearts are not with you? Aren't you tired of watching him after he finishes with you call you an uber or rushes you out. Aren't you tired of her manipulating you with her body to get what she wants? Don't you truly want to be loved? If so heal up and wait on God's perfect timing. Its ok to be on the injured reserved because those on the IR list is still on the team and your coach will let you know when it's time for you to get back in the game of love.

Do you match what you are asking for? Follow the exercises below and let us see if you match what you are asking for.

In the first column, I want you to write down everything you want in a spouse or out of your current spouse... after you have done that I want you to write right beside each trait yes or no; yes, I match it or no, I do not match it. After you have finished both columns, I want you to write how you can improve in that area.

What do you want in a spouse? (Spiritually, emotionally, mentally and physically?	Do you match? Yes or no?	How can you improve in this area?
1		
2		
3		
4		
5		
6		
7		
8		
9		

10		
11		
12		
13		
14		
15		
16		
17		
18		
19		
20		
21		

22		
23		
24		
25		
26		
27		
28		

You cannot be selfless and stuck in your ways at the same time you must have a heart that keeps progressing. Men, the pursuit never stops you have to pursue the new woman she becomes daily, weekly, monthly etc. anyone that is connected to God is being made new daily and if you only pursued her to officially have sex you will be setting yourself up to fail miserably when she is without make up or is sick or gains weight during pregnancy you will be disappointed because you will then be comparing your wife's worst day to every woman's best day at work and then you will have a door open to the enemy to love your wife less and eventually cheat maybe not with your hands but with your heart. There's layers to this thing and if you are not careful you will pursue with the wrong intentions and find yourself falling into a new trap. You must love all of her because she is not going to always to be "beautiful" the way the world defines but she will always be beautiful the way God designed her to be and you must love all of her and pursue her into wifehood, into motherhood, into business-hood into grandmotherhood etc. as she grows your love should grow for her and with her. Having the right perspective now will save your marriage fellas. The same for the women; do not go into your marriage with unrealistic expectations and put so much pressure on your man. You have to be selfless enough to love a man through his fears, failures and faults showing grace when needed and celebrating him as often as you can. It is not easy being a man of God in a sinful world. Do you know how much work and energy it takes to remain faithful as a man? Especially a wanted man? Cherish your good man and celebrate him often because it is not easy. He is going to make mistake but do not make a mountain out of a molehill.

The same way you want him to have a control over his anger and sexual desires the same expectations should be on your emotions and your wondering mind. You are not fit to be a wife if you are more of a knife than a wife. Why so serious? Could it be that women have been indoctrinated with a certain viewpoint of love or maybe could it be that you have been told everything is about you and that all your man is; is a butler? This is not for all women but if the shoe fits deal with that issue because a lot of men's masculinity has be decapitated due to the unnecessary strength of a woman. There is nothing wrong with a strong woman, but her strength must come from God to uphold her man not to tear him down. Because a good God-fearing man is just simply looking for a peaceful place to rest his head. The question is, are you a pillow or are you a stone? The Jezebel spirit is a spirit that wants control it's both male and female and it will creep into relationships and aim to control the union. You have to be mature enough to guard your hearts from this controlling spirit. The marriage can't be only what you want it to be. It's a shared union and you must be open and realistic and not overbearing with a list of this is how I want you to be. Let them be them and you be you and watch the supernatural hand of God do the blending. Its crazy how many people are setting their spouses up to cheat emotionally and mentally. They may not cheat physically but their minds wander to what love could be. You have to be selfless to see correctly. Selflessness seeks to serve the other person everyday through kindness, understanding and grace. There are going to be thousands of mistakes made due to you guys finding a rhythm, but man imagine making those mistakes in a place that is not kind, merciful or gentle. I mean he hasn't been a husband for a month yet and you are already judging him with the standards of a man married 30 years. She hasn't even been a wife for 3 weeks and you are already judging her as if she has been married 40. Chill and let God mold patience into you and understanding. Self-awareness is what leads to selflessness. The number one missile that sinks relationships is selfishness. Selfishness kills relationships selflessness ensures it keeps sailing. Sex thrives in selfless love. Do what it takes to rid lust out of your heart and cut ties with everyone in your sexual past.

In what ways are you selfish?	How could this selfishness sink your relationship?

Have you cut the ties?

Right now, I want you to bring up the names of every person that you deeply loved or love or had a sexual encounter with; how does your soul feel when you hear their name? What thoughts come in mind when you hear their name? Have you truly been freed from them, or are you still tied to them? Because you shouldn't be entertaining another relationship until you have been completely severed away from the other ones. Some people say that the best way to get over someone is to get under someone else and that's the cycle that many people practice. They're trying to use the next sexual experience/ relationship to help them cope with what happened previously. The only person that can help you overcome the ties is Jesus himself. Who are your registered sex offenders and have you forgiven them? Why do you still think about them? What about them is hurting you now. If you do not process these questions, you will not be able to perform well in a marriage.

Let's read some scriptures that will better help us. Matthew 5:28 - *But I say to you that everyone who looks at a woman with lustful intent has already committed adultery with her in his heart.*

God does not just look at sexual acts; he observes sexual intent. Sexual intent is just as bad as sexual acts, because sexual fantasy will lead you to fantasize about how a person feels and with that thought you have already committed a sexual sin against her or him in your heart. If you look at somebody and you wish you could; that's wrong. You must check your heart and ask yourself why when I look at a woman I see a potential sexual partner not a sister in Christ or vice versa? Now, I know it's tough when women wear sexually revealing clothing. In order to be a pure pilgrim passing through you must put the work in privately at home building yourself up in your most holy faith. Doing that will help you be strong and have the right perspective of who the women are out here even if they don't know who they are themselves. And Ladies you got to make sure you understand what being modest means. Not everything should be form-fitted, girls or guys, everything shouldn't be short and up, everything shouldn't be pushed out, because now you're being a part taker in a culture that is hyper-sexualized now that doesn't mean your dress should be determined by the sexual desires of others. But you've got to make sure you are doing as less as you can to provoke. Now don't get me wrong, a lot of guys are turned on even if you're wearing a tablecloth, but what I'm saying is you got to make sure that you're not giving off this sexual energy or sexual enticement, that now has the sexual energy of guys aimed at you. Cover as much as you can because no man of God wants his wife showing everything that should be reserved for his eyes only. Modesty is a mindset for both men and women but if you bypass the mirror of God's word you will definitely let things pass by your natural mirror. The more you are close to God the louder his voice becomes with your modesty.

God cares about lustful intent because lustful intent will eventually turn into lustful action, and lustful action will then turn into a bondage to lust. Your heart is everything. God doesn't measure your habits; he measures your heart. And you got to make sure you clean your heart of all lust so that you won't make it a habit of looking at the other woman lustfully or looking at the other guys lustfully. We become more prone to looking at other people lustfully when we have engaged in lustful things or have been lured away from godly things.

1st Corinthians 6:18 - *Flee from sexual immorality.* Every other sin a person commits is outside the body but the sexually immoral person sins against his body. Flee, insist that there is a severe reason why we must. All other sins are outside of the body, but when we are sexual we are damaging our mind, soul and body. The verse says flee sexual immorality. Sexual immorality is an immoral sexual act, acts that have not been designed by God or are practiced outside a marital covenant. There are sexual encounters, experiences that have been designed by God, originally designed by him within the context of marriage. But some sexual habits or practices have been designed by the perverter himself Satan, and God here says you must flee from them. In order to flee, you've got to have discernment and a deep connection to God without these two you will set yourself up to fail. In order to flee you have to discern the hidden dangers. The wages of sin is death and every encounter you have with another person or with yourself outside of God immediately damages you. You will experience impulses that are unstable, needs that cannot be met and you will develop a mental and an emotional connection to what or who you had sexually encountered. Sexual sin is sweet in the moment but will eventually leave you in a sour place. Your love for God will determine your love for your mind and body. If you are in love with God, you will develop a sense of purpose and that sense of purpose will stabilize your actions because you know you don't have the time to be going through emotional ties with multiple people distracting you from your goals. In order to flee you must have a focus and you must know the facts. You must have a purpose greater than entertaining sexual moments and you must know the facts behind sexual sins effects on your body. The fact that you immediately damage yourself during sexual sin should lead you to flee them.

What do you need to focus on to help you flee?

Hebrews 13:4 - *Let marriage be held in honour among all and let the marriage bed be undefiled for God will judge the sexual immoral adulterers.* That's key. The reason why marriage is not respected is because marriage is not held in honour. We hear more about who's divorcing who then who's been married for 20, 40, 50 plus years. When a marriage is not held in honour, then the components of marriage is not going to be held in honour. If you don't hold marriage in honour, then people will not hold sex in honour. But We have to understand that no matter who holds marriage or sex in honour, God is still going to hold it to his standard and will judge the sexually immoral and adulterers. God is not going to lower his standards on marriage or sex anytime soon. The beautiful thing about the marriage bed is it's undefiled; it's a pure place, it's a holy place, it's a set apart place; that's what the marriage bed was meant for. The marriage bed, the marriage couch, the marriage counter-top, wherever you have sex in your home, that's undefiled, it's set apart, it's holy and it only should be reserved between two married people.

1 John 2:16 - *Love not the world, neither things in the world. For all that's in the world, the desires of the flesh and the desires of the eyes and the pride to make one wise is not from the Father but is from the world.* Love for the world leads to the building up of lust. Before you love something, you've got to be interested in it, and before you are interested in it you must have been influenced some way by it. When Satan influences you, he builds interest, and when you build interest now you begin to love it. But if you love the world and its components, you're only going to build up your lust. What do you love most the things of God or the things of this world?

1 Thessalonians 4:3-5 - *For this is the will of God your sanctification, that you abstain from sexual immorality, that each one of you know how to control his own body in holiness and honour, not in the passion of lust like the Gentiles who do not know God.*

Powerful. The will of God is your sanctification, and it is through sanctification that you learn how to abstain from sexual immorality. God desires for us to know how to initiate self-control through holiness or separation and honour. In order to do all of this, the verse says you have to know God. When you know God, you will know the will of God and when you know God as a person you will know that his will is your sanctification. Sanctification leads you into learning how to abstain from sexual immorality. Sanctification is the process of building spiritual maturity, that the more you become mature through the supernatural work of God that is sanctifying you, cleansing every compartment of you, you will then begin to know how to abstain from sexual immorality and other kinds of sins, because you are no longer being consumed by your desires, you will be more consumed with your determination to know God.

If every day you wake up desiring to know him, you will avoid the pitfalls of the world and you will see the true purpose of Purity. Sexual purity is not a punishment but protection its designed to keep you clear-headed, disease free and emotionally stable. There are so many people who are incapable of going through their days without the effects of their sexual sins. They can't look women in the eyes they can't keep their emotions together they are stalking social media pages all in all keeping them from focusing on the will of God for them that day. Sanctification is a clean sweep meaning you have to have clean systems designed to ensure the process of God stays at work in your life. Healing agents in the body can't do their job if you continue to feed your body chemicals that hinder them the same goes with us being sanctified daily sexually. It's hard for the sanctification process to do its supernatural job if we through ignorance or disobedience continue to feed our souls sexual things. It's up to us to make a decision to abstain meaning to avoid at all cost sexual sin.

The scripture makes a distinction that those who desire holiness will do what it takes to be self-controlled. True freedom is found in restrictions. The more I restrict myself the freer I am. People think freedom is being free without limits buts it's the limits that keeps us free. People who don't know God don't want to know him because they don't want to be "restricted" but it's their lawlessness that's causing them to be bound. God wants us to be able to see the beauty of holiness and honour in our lives. He wants us to feel what it feels like to want sex but not pursue sex or to be so free that you are able to ignore all advances. Your purpose needs a body in order to fulfil it and the state of your body will determine how you perform in your purpose. The devil wants us tied to 3 people, to have 2 kids with another, can't sleep due to a sexual soul tie to an ex he wants us so consumed with sex that we can seek the will of God for our lives. Right now, I am so thankful that I didn't have sex; I get so much done I am able to think clearly I am able to see women as daughters of God. I'm so glad he set me free from pornography because now I don't have to walk around triggered all day or setting myself up to fail in marriage due to unrealistic expectations. When you know God and are self-aware you will do whatever it takes to stay sexually pure.

Colossians 3:5 - *Put to death therefore what is earthly in you, sexual immorality, impurity, passions, evil desires, and covetousness, which is idolatry.* The key phrase in this verse is Put to death what is earthly in you. When something is dead its dead and this verse is giving us a command to put to death what is earthly in us. The only way these earthly things die (sexual immorality, impurity, passions, evil desires, and covetousness) is to starve them. What you feed will lead and those that are saved by God should daily put to death desires the moment they feel them. Your level of maturity and your level of contentment will determine how quickly you put to death what's earthly. It's not easy but it's a must if you want to be successful with God. In order to tap into your full potential with God you have to be intentional. It's going to take accountability, discipline, a sense of purpose and love to at a moment's notice put to death sexual and impure desires. The desires that are listed above are desires of your old man, and they all find their roots in idolatry. Idolatry is loving things or people more than God and when we are not content in who is he to us then those carnal desires will rise. Jesus death on the cross and his resurrection gave us the power through his spirit to put to death these earthly passions. When he is in His rightful place in our hearts all earthly desires will die.

2 Timothy 2:22 - *So flee youthful passions and pursue righteousness, faith, love, and peace along with those who call on the Lord from a pure heart.* Lust is a youthful passion. Mature passions are infused with the things above. Lust is a youthful thing, it's young. If you still engage with lustful things, then it shows that you are immature and still in the elementary stage of the faith. God wants us to grow into maturity because the more mature we are the better we will be in managing the different aspects of his kingdom. It is going to be hard for a pastor to shepherd if he is still struggling with sexual sins; it is going to be hard for an evangelist to share the gospel if she is struggling with insecurities. In order for us to be used at a high level we must flee youthful passions and pursue righteousness or right living, faith, love and peace. When we pursue these things, we will aquire a pure heart. A pure heart is not a perfect heart it's a heart that is perfectly placed in God desiring his will above everything.

Job 31:1 - *I have made a covenant with my eyes. How then could I gaze at a virgin?* Powerful. You've got to make a covenant with your eyes. The first look is not the sin; the second look is. Now I know you have a peripheral vision, there are going to be certain assets that are going to pass through your peripheral vision, and you're going to see it. But your second look or the lack thereof will reveal what kind of heart you have. If you look again, it shows there is something in you that doesn't need to be there anymore. That's why you must make a covenant with your eyes. I rather for you to break your neck to look away than to break your life for still gazing upon. The longer you gaze at something, the longer that look lasts, you will latch on to different things and you will fulfil that sexual desire, whether through pornography or through someone else etc.

Proverbs 6:25 - *Do not desire her beauty in your heart and do not let her catch you with her eyelashes*. Meaning, beauty is vain, do not desire her beauty; desire what makes her truly beautiful; and that's what's on the inside. Beauty is vain; there are a lot of beautiful women, a lot of attractive men who are no good on the inside; good wrapping paper but nothing in the box. In addition, when you are always desiring her beauty and her eyelashes, hips and other assets capture you, then you will soon find yourself in destruction. The same thing for women; if you are overly consumed with his looks and only consumed with what he can provide physically you will too find yourself destroyed

Romans 13:14 - *But put on the Lord Jesus Christ and make no provisions for the flesh to grant further desire*. Keywords in this verse is - make no provisions. You've got to remove all provisions from past, present and potential sins because when you are your weakest you will reach out to whatever you think will help you. As you transition through the sanctification process with God you will see the different layers of your heart. You will see the good the bad and the ugly of you and you will have to make a decision on what systems to implement in your life to ensure you don't make room for sin. We make room for sin when we are not content with God. If we are not careful, we will make provisions to sin we once struggled with, to sins we are struggling with now and will practice habits that will open the door to new sins. That's why it is extremely important to commune with the holy spirit multiple times daily to maintain a fervent spirit. A fervent spirit is a sensitive spirit designed to keep you discerning and seeing things how Christ would see them on earth. Without being cooperative with the Holy Spirit you grant your soul its deepest request. Today think through the past, present and potential sins that may be within arm's reach and take some time to think on how to remove the provision.

In what ways are you providing for the sins below?		
Past Sins:	Present Sins:	Potential Sins:
Provisions:	Provisions:	Provisions:
Plans to stop provisions	Plans to stop provisions	Plans to stop provisions

Psalms 119:9-10 - *How can a young man keep his way pure? By guarding it according to your word. With my whole heart I seek you. Let me not wonder from your commandments.* In order to keep your ways pure your ways must match his word and your whole heart must seek God. The word cleanses, and if we allow it to work on us our ways will become pure.

Mark 7: 20-23 - *What comes out of a person is what defiles him. For from within and out of the heart of a man come evil thoughts, sexual immorality, theft, murder adultery, coveting, wickedness, deceit, sensuality, envy, slander, pride, foolishness.* All these evil things come from within and they defile a person. My question to you from this verse is, what are you allowing to go in you? It's what comes out of you that perverts you. What is your heart like? Some of us, our hearts are dirty and haven't been washed in years. Some of our hearts are worse than some of the dirtiest places on earth. We have sexual thoughts, we want to steal, we want to murder, we want sensuality, we envy, we are prideful, we are foolish and these things are defiling us. Do you want to be successful spiritually, emotionally, physically or do you want to continue to be defiled?

Today you can break this soul tie from sexual immorality. Read the prayer below to break free in the spirit realm, and utilize the questions in this chapter to help you break free in the natural.

Sexual Purity						
How strong is the tie or hold in this area? →				Weak	Mild	Strong
Which areas are affected and in what way? Place a check beside each area that's affected and explain in what way in the larger box below.						
Spiritually	Mentally		Emotionally		Physically	

Heavenly Father I thank you for constantly pursuing me even when I neglected to pursue you. Your love for me overwhelms me and I appreciate you for drawing me to this point of repentance. I desire to walk in purity again and I know through your power I can. Father now I repent of every sexual act including

_____

_____

and I forgive myself and the following people

_____

_____ for sexually abusing me. I accept your forgiveness and freedom now in Jesus name! Through the authority that has been given to me through Christ Jesus I rebuke every demonic spirit of lust, pride, sensuality and fear that is working together to bind me in this area. I sever all sexual ties to the following people

_____

_____

and to the following products

_____

and they no longer have any power over me. I will be untied emotionally, mentally and physically from all partners of my past and from every lustful memory or emotion. My body is now the temple of the Holy Ghost and I will live accordingly. Father I thank you for setting me free today. I will cooperate with your spirit to finish the work in my mind, emotions and body! I appreciate you father for setting me free! My purity journey starts now in Jesus name! Amen!

***

Remember urges are going to rise but the level of those urges are predicated on the environments you entertain. It is not going to be easy to stay pure but you must keep the true identity of the sin in mind and you must constantly stay close to God. He loves you and his spirit will finish its work in you! Stay focused; stay pure!

CHAPTER TEN – MENTAL ILLNESS

God is not the author of Confusion he is the author of clarity. Most if not all of mental illnesses can find themselves rooted in confusion. When people are unaware of who God is and who they are they will fall into pitfalls of mental illness. Many people are trapped within the webs of thought patterns. Thought patterns are caused by a trail of thoughts initiated through influences. You are the complete reflection of the thoughts you allow. Not all your thoughts are your thoughts; some thoughts are demonically inspired meaning they were specifically placed in your mind to spawn a web of confusion. Many of us have given the wrong voices access to our minds. Whatever we allow to pass through our minds will take root in our hearts and eventually be manifested through our hands. God is clear on who he is and who you are and has all the information and processes you need to be set free and to walk in freedom. What the Doctors call mental illness God calls a lack of clarity.

Your mind was designed to protect your heart and these two were designed to stabilize your soul. Your soul houses your mind and your heart. Your mind is supposed to be your filter and your heart is supposed to determine your functions. Your soul (mind and heart) houses various kinds of thoughts they house your memories, emotions, ideas, knowledge and perspectives. Each of these are forms of seeds. Each of us have these forms of thoughts but the question is what quality? The quality of your mind will determine the quality of your life. That's why I try to inspire many people to not think at the level of their negative environment but to think above it because if you can keep your mind afloat your life will eventually reach shore. But when a person allows their mind to sink within the negative lake of their environment their lives will eventually sink. The only solution that can wash our thinking completely clean is the word of God. The highest mind is the Christ mind. Jesus' state of mind was higher than those against him, following him and beneath him he was able like Luke said to discern the hearts of those around him and determine who to entrust himself to. He was able to say the right things at the right time and move accordingly he was thinking 50 moves ahead of everyone and imagine how impactful we could be if we embrace his mind? Right now, you must ask the question who's mind do I have the Christ mind or a carnal mind?

The Christ-like mind is a mind that is renewed; a mind that only goes down a thought-trail toured by the spirit of God. It only adopts mental patterns that keeps it sharp and focused and it's a mind that only sits with things from above. This kind of mind can be had if we are willing to consecrate ourselves. Many of us soak in mental toxins daily and wonder why we cannot operate in the full power of God. A jammed gun can't shoot and how many of us are jammed with unnecessary things keeping us from shooting faith, love, peace etc.? The devil wants your mind… if he can contaminate your mind he can gather the gems of your heart. He doesn't care if you receive Christ he cares mostly if you pursue the Christ mind. He knows how dangerous we are when our minds are totally renewed. He hates when our minds are renewed in regards to sexuality, manhood/womanhood, finances, purpose identity etc. he knows a renewed mind is a mind without weeds. Is your mind full of demonic weeds or divine seeds? Satan knows that a renewed mind has the greatest reach and possess a ton of resources. That's why he goes through great lengths to ensure his system is in every person's home. He wants what my mom calls the one-eyed demon your tv, phone, tablet etc. in every home that is connected to channels and ideas that can stifle the renewing process of God keeping minds operating at a poor level. If he can ensure that the "believers" time is mostly used compromising than consecrated, he can keep them from reaching deep into his territories providing solutions.

The quality of your mind matters to God. How do you think? How do your memories affect you, how stable are your emotions, what ideas are you funding through your energy, what knowledge are you after and how do you see what you see? Answering these questions will reveal the state of your mind.

What are your dominant thoughts right now?	What is at the end of these trails of thoughts?	How can you turn these negative thoughts into positive ones?

What are your significant memories?	How are they affecting you?	How can you remember these memories differently and use them as motivation?
What are your dominant emotions right now?	What triggers these emotions?	What do you need to do to stabilize these emotions?

What ideas are you entertaining right now and why?	How much of your energy is going towards your God-given ideas?	What do you need to do to focus more on your God-given ideas?
Would you consider yourself a wise person? Why or why not?	What knowledge are you not applying right now that you need to apply?	What do you need to do to transition from being a hearer to a doer?

How do you see and how should you see the following?	
How you see	How should you see
Yourself	
Your significant other or the opposite sex?	
God	
Time	
Resources + $	

Sex	
Work + Ministry + Business	
Spiritual Warfare + Resistance	
People	
Those above and beneath you	
Leadership + Serving	

Mental Acknowledgements – Emotional Attachments.

The best way for a person to be soul tied to something or someone negatively is to ensure they acknowledge it mentally and eventually become emotionally attached. The Bible says in Proverbs to trust the Lord with all your heart, lean not onto your own understandings but in all your ways acknowledge him and he will straighten out your path. This scripture speaks volumes to mental illnesses. Now let me preference my comments I am not a doctor and I'm not a licensed psychiatrist but what I have noticed throughout my interactions with people is that most people who struggle with a mental illness their mental illness was spawned by some kind of significant moment or specific demonic interference that is leading them to accept or acknowledge their mental illness. People have given a lot of their wellbeing to the diagnosis of a doctor who was only taught to medicate and not to heal. Many doctors are influenced by the desire for money or by what they were taught. A diagnosis has a significant weight on the mind; when a doctor says you have _____ people see their diagnosis as the highest source of info and seeing that a lot of people are not deeply connected to God or disciplined they listen to what the doctor says never consulting God and begin to say the diagnosis out of their mouths. When you say I have ADHD you are now giving a demon the legal right to ensure you operate under that title. That's why you must be careful what you say because a miss diagnosis repeated out of your mouth gives legal right to a demon to manifest that illness. It's like telling a person who has a history of stealing they can enter your home when you are not there but when they take from you; you get mad like you didn't give them permission. We have been conditioned to hear, think, speak, and act in a certain way constantly giving demons the legal right to interfere with our minds. They want chaos in your life and the best way to do so is through confusion and demonically inspired confessions. We are supposed to trust God with all of hearts not some but all and to not lean on our own other peoples understandings as support but to in all of our significant ways acknowledge him and he will straighten our paths. What have you acknowledged and what are you emotionally attached too because anything that has an emotional attachment to you will become your leader.

What mental illnesses or negative things are you acknowledging out of your mouth and how are they affecting your life in a negative way?	What phrases could you replace these negative diagnosis or sayings with?

We can only acknowledge at the level of how we perceive ourselves. There are only three areas of perception too low, too high and biblically. When a person perceives below how they should biblically they will only acknowledge the negative or become a low-grade individual. When a person perceives himself or herself, more highly than they ought they will climb into ego and pride and will only acknowledge their own strength and desires but when people grow into perceiving themselves in a biblically balanced way then they will only acknowledge what is true. What you acknowledge, accept, adopt or adapt to will eventually become your way of life. So many people are attaching themselves mentally to things that are taking root in their hearts and affecting their behaviours and their health. What you acknowledge you will answer to. The enemy wants you to only answer to the one thing that is the sole cause to the soul-tie of your heart. Satan has a well-oiled machine at his disposal enlisting demons, individuals and microorganisms to be your taskmaster they want you mentally stuck in depression, oppression, regret, selfish ambition etc. instead of in the things of God. He knows that if your mind is weak, your body will become vulnerable. A woman with a weak mind will always find herself looking for validation and acceptance and one wrong man at the right time will captivate her mind and lure her into a compromised state and she will find herself with either a weaker mind or a baby in her womb.

Romans 8:5-6 - *For those who live according to the flesh set their minds on the things of the flesh. But those who live according to the spirit set their minds on the things of the spirit. For to set the mind on the flesh is death but to set the mind on the spirit is life and peace.* Your lifestyle is a reflection of your mindset. Wherever your mind sits will determine the style of life you will live. A lot of people have their minds set on the things of the flesh not realizing that when you have your mind set on its carnal state it will only produce carnality. It is our responsibility to make sure we set our minds on the things of the spirit. Now don't get me wrong, the world is going to make it extremely tough for you to do that, but you've got to make sure you set the right environment, the right culture in your life to make sure you have clarity; you've got to set a culture of clarity. Culture is everything. What kind of culture have you set for your life? Because whatever culture you allow to cultivate in your life will determine what type of mindset you will have. When you have the right culture, a Godly culture with Godly community, with Godly television, Godly radio, Godly podcasts, Godly influences, then you don't ever have to worry about your mind being set on the things of the flesh. If all you hear or watch is pornography, lust, greed, selfish ambitions then your mind is going to follow those influences. If your mind is always hearing business, business, business, work, work, work, don't sleep, don't sleep, don't sleep, drink, drink, drink, sex, sex, sex then you're going to end up having that type of life. What culture is cultivating you?

What kind of culture is in your life? Take some time to list what you do regularly and beside the questions circle if it is a positive or negative influence and write down how it is helping or hurting you.

But first what kind of culture would you like to have in your life?		
What do you watch regularly	+ or -	**How is it helping or hurting you?**
What do you listen to regularly	+ or -	**How is it helping or hurting you?**

Who are the people you admire the most? (Famous/ non famous)	+ or -	How are they helping or hurting you?
Who are your closest friends?	+ or -	How are they helping or hurting you?
Where do you visit to the most? + What are in these environments?	+ or -	How is this place helping or hurting you?

What thoughts occupy your mind the most?	+ or -	How are they helping or hurting you?

What emotions occupy your heart the most	+ or -	How are they helping or hurting you?

After working through this exercise what kind of culture did you have in your life and what do you need to do to set the right culture in your life?

What kind of culture did you have →	Good	Eh	Or Bad
What do you need to do to create the culture you want in your life both externally and internally?			

God wants us to have a balanced mind. Yes, there is work, and yes, there is time for play, but how do you work and how do you play? It all boils down to the culture you set for your life. Setting your mind on the spirit leads to life in peace; setting your mind on the flesh leads to death and anxiety. Which one do you want? If you set your mind on the spirit even though it may seem rigid and requires more discipline, you will ultimately have peace if you do it the right way. If you pursue the woman the right way, if you allow yourself to be pursued the right way, if you wait until marriage, then you will have a peaceful outcome. Do you know there is a set peace waiting for you all you have to do is listen and follow the ways of God? Following the spirit always guarantees peace but following the flesh will always lead to stress and anxiety. Do you not see the correlations? That if I do the things of the world I will have anxiety. If I have sex with a girl, I am probably going to have anxiety wondering if she's pregnant or not. Or if I do get a woman pregnant, now I have unnecessary stress in my life because one it could be a crazy girl that I have a baby with, or two I now have a child in the world prematurely. Following the flesh will always cripple you it boasts of a good time but will always leave you with regrets. I promise you there is not one person who did it God's way that has regrets. Be careful where you set your mind!

Colossians 3:2 - *Set your mind on the things that are above, not on the things that are on the earth. If you set your mind on things above, you will be above. If you set your mind on things below you will remain below.* Isn't it heaven where we are trying to go? The goal is to think like they think up there, to think how God thinks. We are to be thinking above - thinking above pornography, thinking above sex outside of marriage, thinking above lying, thinking above gossip, thinking above, living above, doing above what is carnal. How many people are far below where they are supposed to be today? Whatever you engage in today will determine how high you are tomorrow. So many people are still at the bottom of the pile, not because of God but because of their decisions. When you set your mind on the things above and on what's righteousness, you will eventually be there. You will never be higher than where your mind is set. You determine the altitude. Wherever your mind is your life will go - as a man thinks in his heart so is he. If you think on the things above, you will be above. Thinking on the level of this carnal world is a waste of time don't you want to think how God thinks don't you want the highest mindset?

Romans 12:1-2 - *I beseech you therefore brothers by the mercies of God that you present your bodies as a living sacrifice holy and acceptable to God, which is your spiritual worship. Do not be conformed to this world but be transformed by the renewing of your mind that by testing you may discern what is the will of God, what is good and acceptable and perfect.* In order to become successful in the things of God, we have to become a living sacrifice, living and dying simultaneously. Becoming a living sacrifice means something must die while something is living. He says, 'I beseech you therefore brothers by the mercies of God that you present your bodies.' It's not saying you have a choice but that you present your bodies as a living sacrifice, holy and acceptable to God which is your spiritual worship. A living sacrifice says I am sacrificing the carnal man and giving the renewed man the opportunity to live, to thrive, to win. Every day I must present my body to God as a useful resource. My question to you is are you useful or useless? It all boils down to which one of you is living. Right now which one is the most alive your renewed self or your carnal self?

The bible talks about how God is looking for a people that will worship him in spirit and in truth. Worship how we see it today is expressed worship not embodied worship. Embodied worship can manifest into expressive worship but expressive worship is worthless to God he even said that people honour him with their lips, but their hearts are far from him. God measures the heart. Spiritual worship is an embodied worship meaning that your day to day life both hidden and public is worship to God. Quiet obedience is a better sounding worship than a thousands of people at a "worship" concert. God looks at intent not expression. Anyone can run, jump, lift their hands and shout but not everyone obeys immediately. God is looking for immediately not eventually. Does your day to day activities both private and publicly honour God or the god of this world?

Our holiness and our acceptability is not predicated on our works but on the work of Jesus. Believing and accepting the work of Jesus sets us apart and makes us acceptable; this becomes our true worship. I don't have to work to be accepted; I have already been accepted. Our conformity and our transformation is predicated on the direction our minds are going. The Bible reads do not be conformed to this world but be transformed by the renewing of your mind. Just like the rudder on a ship turns a huge boat, the same is with the mind. If I listen to a person long enough and I analyse how that person thinks I can easily predict that person's future. That's why I must make sure that my mind does not stay still or stays in carnality because carnality leads to conformity. Many people have allowed their minds to rot, to be wasted, to be stagnant, to the point that all of a sudden, they believe in what the doctor says or they allow these different things to clutter their minds and confuse them, then all of a sudden their lives sinks. But when a person's mind has been turned in the right direction then eventually their life will slowly follow. You can tell the way a person thinks by the results of their life. My question to you is, where is your life today? Because your life follows your thinking patterns.

There is a big difference between transaction and transformation. People want transaction but not transformation. The reason why many people cannot birth the fruits of a renewed mind is because they only go to God for transactional purposes, they don't go to God to be transformed; there is a big difference. Many people care about the presents he has versus the presences he gives. His presence is what we should look for but most people are so caught up in what they want out of life that they miss out on the life or the abundant life that Christ wants to give. So, if you continue to go to God for a transactional experience you will realize you're going to the wrong god. But when you want transformation, you will truly be transformed.

Your mind was designed to test what the will of God is for you daily; it was designed to test what is good, acceptable and perfect. If your mind is poor, you will not be able to test or discern the will of God. If your mind is poor you won't even know what is good, because a lot of things that look good, taste good, feels good, seems good, are not good. And if you do not have a rich mind and your mind is poor you won't know what's acceptable and perfect. The will of God is key, you have to have a sharp mind to be able to know what the will of God is, not just the big will but the little wills everyday. What's the will of God for me in this situation or that situation? The more your mind is trained the quicker you will be able to respond and the quicker you will be able to engage with the will of God for every specific moment of your life. You will know when the spirit of God tells you to talk to a person a little bit longer, you will know the will of God when God tells you to call your mom, you will know the will of God when God says give that person on the side of the road $5. Many people get so caught up in what's the ultimate will of God for them, but they don't want to seek out what's the will of God for them daily. When you follow the will of God daily you will eventually stumble into his ultimate will for your life. You've got to have the mind of Christ to know what is truly good.

It's not our bad choices that messes us up it's sometimes the "good decisions". The bulk of our problems lie not between good and bad but between good and God. We must make sure we decipher between what's God and what's good. There are a lot of great opportunities, a lot of good opportunities; but not all good opportunities are God opportunities that's why we have to have the right type of mind sharp enough to know what God's will for us is truly. Is your mind conforming or transforming?

Colossians 2:8 says - *See to it that no one takes you captive by philosophy and empty deceit according to human tradition, according to the elemental spirits of the world and not according to Christ.* Christ should be so captivating to you that nothing will have the opportunity to hold you captive. It is our responsibility to ensure that we process everything that comes into our mind, that we take captive every philosophy if it isn't the philosophies of Christ. That's why it is important for you to seek truth for yourself. Do not take my word for it concerning my faith. It is your responsibility to search your faith out and to see what is true, because when you have discerned, processed, researched what is to be true you will have a greater chance of being committed to it. If you don't know if it is true, if it's just a philosophy, if it's just another person's opinion then you can find yourself captive to a lie or potentially drawn away from the truth because you didn't make the truth true to you.

How many people right now are supporting a lie? There are millions of people who believe in different religions that are lies. There are a lot of people who are in relationships connected by lies. And it's crazy how no one takes the time to process through all philosophies and every deceit. This world is full of deceptive opinions and Satan's deception is everywhere. We cannot allow deception to rule us; that's why it is important for you to find the truth about health, the truth about wealth, the truth about relationships, the truth about everything so that you won't follow empty deceits. Everything deceptive at its core is empty meaning it produces nothing. It is like biting into a hollow apple expecting it to be a real apple; it's empty, it's not what it is perceived to be. Behind every lie is a truth. Find the truth!

Also, you've got to be very careful that you don't follow human traditions. One of the things that keep people from a heavenly commitment are earthly traditions or human traditions. Many people are more committed to traditions created by men than pursuing the truth given by God. It's our responsibility to make sure that we are not bound by or held captive to philosophies, empty deceits, human traditions and things that birth itself from the demonic spirits of this world. Everything must be compared to the truth that is why you have to know Christ for yourself, because if you know Christ for yourself and you are captivated by that truth, you will not find yourself captured by anything else. My question to you is what are you mostly committed to? Are you committed to people's YouTube philosophies, professors' philosophies, your pastors' philosophies? Are you committed to deceits that are empty and hollow? Are you committed to human traditions more than you are to God?

You have to be like Shadrach Meshach and Abednego that stood for the truth. When everyone else was bowing to a lie they stood for the truth. While everyone else was following the king's petition against prayer Daniel stayed committed. You've got to stay committed no matter what because that's when you will see salvation come through at its best. If you are not committed to God you cannot expect God to be committed to you, meaning if you are over here living contrary to his ways you can't expect him to always deliver you from consequences and situations. But if he knows your heart is genuinely committed then God will supernaturally provide for you. You can have the whole nation in awe of you watching you stand while everyone else bows. You can have everyone concerned about you as you are in the lion's den, but God will always come through for those who are committed to Him; but you have to know the truth of Christ in order to stay committed.

2 Corinthians 10:5 ³ For though we walk in the flesh, we are not waging war according to the flesh. ⁴ For the weapons of our warfare are not of the flesh but have divine power to destroy strongholds. ⁵ We destroy arguments and every lofty opinion raised against the knowledge of God, and take every thought captive to obey Christ, ⁶ being ready to punish every disobedience, when your obedience is complete.

It is important for us to understand the word captive. Instead of us being made captive we must capture any and everything that arises in our minds. Our minds must have the right filters and must be disciplined. We fall into captivity when we do not have godly processes or systems. It is our responsibility to take every thought captive. This is impossible when we do not have a disciplined mind. A disciplined mind is the fruit of matured disciples of Jesus. A mature follower of Jesus is able to destroy arguments and every lofty opinion due to where their disciplined mind is positioned. The height of your mindset is predicated on the teachers you follow. It's hard to bind an individual who is thinking above the levels of those trying to bind them. It's hard because they are in tuned mostly with their creator than what's been created.

I always give the example of the people in the Federal Reserve, the people who are responsible for America's currency. These Individuals do not waste their time studying the fakes, because the fakes are made new every day, but an original is made new once. Since the original is made new once, all they have to do is study the original $20 bill, the original $50 bill, the original $100 bill, etc., they study these so much and become so knowledgeable of the original that even the smallest of differences that's brought their way as counterfeits they are able to spot it. That's how we are supposed to be. The reason why many people have strongholds in their mind, number one they don't have any knowledge of God, number two they don't have any discipline in their lives, and number three they are unwilling to study, to show themselves approved. Many people get so consumed with everything else, the lies, the fakes, they'd rather study the Illuminati, they'd rather study the devil that changes than the God that never changes. If you study the devil, the devil is crafty, but God is concrete. Therefore, what happens is many people begin to pursue the devil or are in the witch-hunt to the point that they are following/ chasing all of these fakes not knowing that the fakes constantly change, and since the fakes constantly change, they will always find themselves confused. However, when you know God and you know him to be true, then you will be able to be set free and be able to capture everything immediately that comes to your ear gate or eye gate.

Nothing that does not belong to God or adheres to anything Godly should not get beyond the gates of your ears or your eyes. We're not talking about just your outer ears or eyes; we're talking about your inner ear and eye as well. Negative thoughts should not even be allowed to pass. In certain banks, in certain places, there are barriers beyond the initial entrance. Now, you can walk through the main entrance of a bank, but there is a security gate that keeps people from going deeper into where the safe is. You may have access to go into a certain building, but you don't have access to go completely into where the safe is. We have to make sure that even though we hear things that the guard at the inner gate, which is the Holy Spirit, is able to check the ID, to see who does this thought identifies itself with. If it does not identify itself with God, love, joy, peace and the Holy Ghost, if it does not belong or identify with Him then it should be removed immediately.

When a person walks into a bank shady immediately, there are eyes on that person. If a person is trying to do criminal activity and the officer is aware, that person would be held captive, detained, processed, thoroughly examined before that person can come back again. You've got to put restraining orders on certain thoughts. You've got to make sure that they can't even come within 20 miles of you regarding your heart. They may be able to come through radio waves, television waves, podcasts, music and songs, but you've got to make sure it's not going to come within any area of your heart. Many people's minds are so clogged with unnecessary things because they don't know Christ, or they are not allowing him to take those thoughts captive. It is your responsibility to hold those things captive and let the spirit of God process and push out the door those philosophies.

Isaiah 26:3, the Bible says, *You keep him in perfect peace whose mind is stayed on you because he trusts in you*. Trusting in God is a hard thing, it's like trusting in something you can't see. But it is crazy how we trust in things we can't see every day. We trust in air; we are breathing something we cannot physically see, but its presence is tangible. Perfect peace is what we should be after, the peace that surpasses all understanding. All understanding meaning that there may be different things that may come my way but I have a peace that surpasses it. The only way you get this perfect peace is when your mind is stayed on him. When Peter stepped off the boat, even during the storm, he had peace because his eyes was stayed on Christ. But the moment he took his eyes off Jesus what was catastrophic and chaotic around him took precedence on his peaceful moment even during the storm. That's why the Bible says you keep him in perfect peace. God's responsibility is to keep you in perfect peace; your responsibility is to keep your mind on him and His responsibility is to keep you in a perfect peace. If you want to be kept you have to keep your mind on him. And when a person does that, that person survives and even in the midst of storms they will find peace.

I love the words 'perfect peace'. Perfect peace means the right amount of peace for your specific situation to keep you as calm as needed if you choose to be. God doesn't immediately give us what we ask for, but he does immediately give us a peace to assure us that he has heard. Do you trust him for your specific situation? I Know its not easy for your mind to remain stable during tough times. Sometimes we lose the battle in our minds due to how tough our lives become. It takes a lot of mental toughness to keep our minds stayed on God during tough times but it's a must for us because the enemy is not going to stop sending darts at our minds he is going to always bring up and ex, a memory or a tormenting thought to see if he can take your mind off of God. Anxiety builds when we take our minds off God. Stress builds when we try to do God's job for ourselves. Satan knows that where the presence of God is there is peace and peace assures and if he can get you away from God he can then rob you of assurance. Do you know how many people worry for no reason? God has answered their prayers but seeing that they are not mentally tough they take their minds off of God and worry. Why worry when you have his peaceful assurance. No matter what keep your mind on Him.

2 Timothy 1:7 - *For God gave us a spirit, not of fear but of power and love and self-control.* Many people are bound because of fear, the lack of love and the lack of self-control. A lot of people find themselves bound mentally, number one by fear. Fear has an acronym, I said it earlier in the book - false evidence appearing real. Many people have allowed fear to become the crux keeping them from walking in faith. I say walking in fear and walking in place is the same thing; you end up nowhere. A lot of people's minds have been halted, hindered, kept from pursuing the things of God because they are afraid. Many people have allowed fear to keep them from executing in power. Faith is power. The enemy responds to power; he doesn't respond to just mere words, he responds to words of power. And if you are afraid to speak life, then you will give him the opportunity to present death. You've got to execute in power, you've got to say right now "my mind is clear through the authority of Christ I have mental clarity, I am not ADHD, I am not ADD, I do not have a mental illness, I'm not going to allow my mind to be tormented, I know who I am in Christ and He will liberate me mentally." You do not walk in fear. If you walk in fear and you take the diagnosis then you are not going to be able to walk in power, you are not going to have power to break those strongholds because you don't have enough belief. You've got to build your faith in order to execute in faith.

God's faith is not predicated on the quantity of faith but the quality of faith. There are people who have a mustard seed type faith who execute better and with more power than someone who looks like they have a multitude of faith. People can look like they have faith, but when their faith is tested it's been proven to be null and void. Faith is power. Power means submission, submitting to the supernatural work of the Holy Spirit daily. In order for me to execute in power daily I've got to trust in a supernatural power; daily. The reason why many people are battling today is because they think they are powerless. I am talking about believers, they think they are powerless. They have allowed themselves to be weakened even though they have been enlisted on a winning team.

And love, a lot of people are bound mentally because they lack love. You don't have to be surrounded by love if you have been filled with love through God on the inside. God loves you more than anyone on the planet and his love is powerful enough to help you conquer anything. Do you know how many average people accomplished above average things because they were loved? Love validates it reassures and many people are settling for mental illnesses, for bad relationships because they are completely aware of how loved they are. There is no fear in love for perfect love cast out fear. When we meet Gods perfect love and we relentlessly stay in that presence of love we will accomplish the impossible. There is nothing wrong with desiring human love but there is a love that is greater and that is the love of God. Because I am loved by him I work hard for him because he loved me I obey and no one can tell me Josh you are not a good speaker or Josh you suck at what you do I know who I am and I know who called me period. When you know who you are in Him you will do exploits. Do you truly know how loved you are? Your actions will let you know.

Self-Control

Many people lack discipline. Discipline is essential for success. In order for us to succeed we must allow God to discipline us, so that he can give us his self-control. In order for us to walk in the spirit we must be fed and supplied by the fruits of the spirit. Fruit gives energy, when a person eats fruit it energizes them, it helps them to flourish, it gives them the nutrients they need. In order for us to be able to walk in the spirit we have to be fed and supplied by the fruit of the spirit. We have to be fed with joy, we have to be fed with love, we have to be fed with patience, and we are only fed those things if we are plugged into the vine which is Jesus. Do you believe that? Do you believe you have power? Do you believe you're loved? And are you willing and asking for self-control?

1 Peter 5:8, the Bible says, *Be sober minded, be watchful. Your adversary the devil prowls around like a roaring lion seeking someone to devour.* In order to be watchful you have to be sober minded. In order for the enemy to not gain a hold on you, you must be sober enough to discern. Sober minded means a mind that's not intoxicated, a mind that's not overly intrigued, a mind that's not consumed with ideologies. A sober mind is a still mind, a mind at peace. It's like drinking, it's hard for a person that's intoxicated with alcohol to discern and to be watchful. They're in a different level of looseness that they're not able to have a sound enough mind to discern what's going on. Many people have lost their virginity because of alcohol, many people have fallen into sexual habits because of alcohol, many people have gotten into fights because of alcohol, and, many people have gotten into car accidents or have died or have killed people because of alcohol, due to that person not being sober-minded.

Your level of sober mindedness will determine your level of discernment, and if you're not sober minded and your mind is overly intoxicated with anxiety, overly intoxicated with stress, overly intoxicated with fear, overly intoxicated with success and being driven you will find yourself in situations that will spawn negative consequences affecting you for years. If you're not sober minded, then the devil will be able to devour you. People who are not watchful or alert are easily devoured. Many people let's take for instance being driven, they're so driven to be successful that they're not watchful of the pride, arrogance and greed that's building up in their heart. Yes, being driven is good, but you must be sober minded behind the wheel. A lot of people are doing certain things being rushed and going fast and are not being present enough to see what's being presented to them. That's why the Bible says you have to be sober minded, you have to still your mind. Now how do you still your mind? You carve out a space where you can go to God regularly with no distractions to be still.

In order to hear from God you've got to have a still life. In order to have a still life you have to have a still mind. The mind is the engine that causes the life to be floored, meaning overly driven, pressed, and overly stressed. That's why it's your responsibility to say you know what I'm not going to allow my life to go faster or, beyond the point where God has it. I'm going to remove all distractions - if that means I've got to get off social media, if that means I have to delete these apps and delete this and cut these friends off, or be single for a while I will, you've got to remove anything that's causing impulsiveness and clutter in your mind so that you're able to hear clearly.

If your mind is not sober you will be devoured. It says *Your adversary the devil prowls around like a roaring lion seeking someone to devour*. That means your enemy is always on his job; he's sober minded. Those demons assigned to you are sober minded, they are highly aware, hyper-alert on how to make you fall. He prowls around like a roaring lion seeking someone to devour. I like where the text says 'like a roaring lion' - that means he's roaring to see how you respond. He allows that lust to roar loud in your mind to see how you'll respond to it. He allows that girl to roar, that guy to roar, that business to roar, he lets it roar to see how you respond. Are you going to speak back to it with power and authority because you're sober minded? Or are you just going to lay down and let it devour you? The enemy will use any and everything to roar its loudest, to get you to forsake and lean into his devouring. Remember he's all roar no bite.

I want the enemy to be so thrown that when he comes into my life, it takes him weeks and weeks and weeks to develop a plan because I'm always sober minded. When a person is sober minded, they are watchful when the thief comes. Everything becomes unprotected when a person is not sober minded. How is your mind today? Is it sober? Or is it intoxicated?

1 John 4:1 - *Beloved do not believe every spirit, but test the spirits to see whether they are from God, for many false prophets have gone out into the world*. 'Do not believe every spirit' proves that there are bad spirits; and that we must test the spirits. The Bible talks about when Jesus was walking around he didn't entrust himself to everyone because he knew their hearts. That's what we must do when it comes to testing spirits. Many people wrestle with flesh and blood but are not discerning the spirit that's igniting the fight. You've got to say in every situation, "Is there a spirit at work behind this individual?

How do I test the spirit?

You test the spirit by number one, looking at the actions of a person. If a person is acting irrational chances are there could be a spirit, there. I'm not saying every situation has a spirit, but you test it by looking to see if this is a rational or irrational presentation? Is this an overly emotional or a poised situation? Because the devil is going to try to always get you into impulsiveness, to get you excited, heightened, or to get you focused more on your emotions than your mind. He wants you to feel offended, he wants you to feel upset, he wants you to get offended, because he knows when a person is offended they're going to try and prove themselves - you don't have to prove yourself. Never let someone's insecurity weaken your securities. The enemy wants you to always engage with their pawns so that you too will look like a fool or potentially be involved with something that will leave consequences in your life.

You must test the spirit by its emotional stability. That's why knowing the word of God mentally and trusting it emotionally in the heart realm is essential for you to be successful. If you do not allow the two to work together you're going to fail in every battle that you face. Both must be strengthened, you have to have emotional stability and you have to have mental clarity in order to succeed.

Test every spirit by discernment, the word of God and not engaging until you know. Do not engage deeply in any relationship until you know who sent this person into your life. If God did not send this person to be your wife, then there's no need to even be intimate/ best friends with that person. That's why everything that comes before me I always ask in my heart to the Holy Spirit, "Who is behind this person? Who is sending this person or opportunity? God are you sending this? If you're sending it confirm it. If you didn't send it then have them to expose themselves." Like with any test you need to know the material in order to be successful with the test. If you don't know the material of the word of God, if you're not engaged with God, how will you be able to test the spirits to see if it is of God?

Psalms 119:34 says - *Give me understanding that I may keep your law and observe it with my whole heart.* The reason why many of us are where we are is due to us not wanting to consult God. God is not just a rule giver; he is also one who will give reasons why. I love what Psalm 119 says; it says give me understanding. That right there lets us know what kind of heart this person has. He says, "God I must have understanding in order to keep your law and preserve it with my whole heart." The reason people don't follow God is because they have been misinformed. When a person truly understands why waiting until marriage for sex is important, when a person truly understands then they're going to do their best to keep it and to observe it. But if a person has only been told sex is bad, sex is wrong when sex is actually a good thing then their curiosity will build and they will try and test it out for themselves.

Instead of telling people that they shouldn't; we must tell them why they shouldn't. God wants us to give people understanding. Not through a sternness or strong tone, but in love, in patience, in helping them process, in getting their minds to understand. Because when a person has understanding or a heart to understand they will grow.

Hebrews 13:8 - *Jesus Christ is the same yesterday, today and, forever*. God is immutable meaning that he never changes. This should comfort us seeing that he remains consistent. Knowing that Jesus is consistent should give us a mental peace, that if I know that he's true and alive then I know I can trust everything that was said about him and everything that he has said about himself and about me. If he never changes then his principles never change and if his principles never change then the results or the rewards of those principles never change.

That's why I'm confident that I'm anchored to a God who never changes, because if the principles don't change then I know the promises won't change. Those who follow this formula are always rewarded. Those who truly love God as a person and love him beyond everything else and follow his principles out of love because God is love, then they will always get to enjoy the promises. I'm thankful that he never changes.

John 16:13 - *When the spirit of truth comes he will guide you into all the truth, for he will not speak of his own authority but whatever he hears he will speak, and he will declare to you the things that are to come*. I love this scripture. Jesus was telling his disciples that I'm about to die I'm about to go but, I'm going to send the comforter the Spirit of God to you, the spirit of truth - that means the most honest entity on this planet, the surest thing on this earth. Surer than a dictionary, surer than google, surer than anything on earth. He was saying that the spirit of truth will guide you into all truth, and he will not speak of his own authority, but whatever he hears he will speak, and he will declare to you the things that are to come. That's why you got to test every spirit because every spirit is connected to a kingdom and every kingdom is connected to a king. If you don't test the spirit, then you may be confused or could be used to advance the wrong kingdom for the wrong king. That's why it's important for you to know the spirit - is this the truthful spirit? Does this come from the spirit of truth or the spirits of lies?

Isaiah 40:31 - *But they who wait for the Lord shall renew their strength. They shall mount up with wings like eagles, they shall run and not be weary, they shall walk and not faint.* Many people are bound mentally because they lack the awareness of patience and timing. They look at the word 'wait' in Isaiah 40:31 as sitting down doing nothing. They look at it as absolutely doing nothing. But what they fail to realize is that the word wait means to serve - my strength is renewed when I serve the Lord. It's not renewed meaning waiting on the Lord as far as on a park bench, but it is strengthened through serving him. This will enable me to mount up, run, and walk – in other words it will lure me into action. See these are action words. For me to mount up, to run, to walk and not lose energy I must be supernaturally strengthened. The reason why many people are not mounting and flying like eagles, running and not growing weary, walking and not fainting is because they're not renewing their strength. In order for you to maintain mental clarity, you have to renew your strength constantly, and you can only renew your strength by serving God - serving God privately and publicly. Serving God meaning, "God I'm here to serve. What else can I do to help?" Publicly I'm going to serve my church, my local community; I'm going to serve, serve, serve. Because in my servanthood I'm strengthened, in my serving-hood I'm made mature, so that when it's time to advance to the next level and to manage it, I will be able to.

We have to trust in his timing. His timing is sure, his love is sure, and he wants you to serve him so that you can be strengthened. I want you to repeat this prayer after me as you read and embrace your freedom

The Mind						
How strong is the tie or hold in this area? →				Weak	Mild	Strong
Which areas are affected and in what way? Place a check beside each area that's affected and explain in what way in the larger box below.						
Spiritually		Mentally	Emotionally		Physically	

Prayer:

Heavenly Father I am thankful that you have given me through your son Jesus the ability to have his mind. Through you I can have the same mind-set, the same mental clarity, and the same discernment Jesus had when he walked on this earth. I repent for the following sins that opened the door for confusion to come in

_____

_____

and I sever all ties and allegiances to all forms of mental illnesses. I cancel every curse I have spoken over myself and I cancel every curses that was spoken over me by others. I no longer have the following mental illnesses

_____

_____ in my life

and I walk in clarity in every areas of my life in Jesus name. Demons in the name of Jesus I rebuke you and declare your plots to be cancelled and I command you to leave my life and my mind alone right now in Jesus name! I have the mind of Christ and I think, speak and discern like him. Leave my mind for good in Jesus Name.

Father I thank you for covering me as your spirit leads me into greater depths of freedom. Help me with my words lord and help me with my thinking. I fill this temple up now with your word and will be a useful servant to you. I thank you again! Amen!

In order to have this freedom, you have to remove all negative influences today. You've got to make sure you surround yourself with positive energy, positive vibes, positive people, and protect your mind. A mind is a terrible thing to waste. The sad thing is a lot of people are wasting it every day; but not you in Jesus name. Continue to go over the exercises in this chapter and stay with Jesus!

CHAPTER ELEVEN – PRIDE AND VANITY

There's nothing wrong with being proud of where you're from, what you have accomplished, or proud of your heritage or your family, but this state of proudness becomes perverted when it becomes your identity. Pride is one of the number one things that keeps us from succeeding spiritually, the number one thing that keeps us from being set free. If you look at the word pride you see two letters I-D. ID represents identification. Most people's proudness becomes perverted when they begin to identify themselves with where they're from, what they've accomplished, their family, who they are, etc. Whoever you identify with determines what you are most proud of or mostly consumed with. Do not think of yourself too highly, think of yourself accurately. We must always see ourselves considering who Jesus is, what he has accomplished and what he desires to do in us. All of us fall short in comparison to Him.

Our pride grows when we compare ourselves to others; our pride diminishes when we compare ourselves to God. The best way to stay humble is to compare ourselves vertically not horizontally. It is essential for you and me to daily compare ourselves to Christ, because when we compare ourselves to Christ there will always be room to improve. If Christ is who I identify with, if Christ is who I'm searching for then my pride will turn into humility immediately. But when people compare themselves to other people they begin to have either an arrogant or a self-hatred heart. That's why the Bible says that making comparisons with others is not wise because no one is made the same and each person is different. But when you are already identified with Christ you're somebody because of him. You're not somebody because of you; you're not somebody because of what you've accomplished, you're not somebody because of whatever else. You are who you are by the grace of God, the grace that was presented to us through the life, death, burial and resurrection of Jesus. That's why it's essential for you and me not to think of our self-more highly than we ought to think or lowly but we must think of ourselves accurately, and the only way we can look at ourselves accurately is if we ingratiate ourselves in God and know who we are on this totem pole.

Anytime you begin to compare yourself to anything else to determine your worth you're now telling that thing you give me significance and worth. The reason why people hold onto these things is because these things make them feel like somebody and gives them a false sense of worth. What are you holding on to, using it as an identification card to give you access? Many people try to say well since I went to this school I'm proud and since I went to this school and got this degree, this is my identification card to get me where I got to go. This is my ID card, my pride, to get me access. But the thing about God is when I identify with him, he will take me places that a degree can't take me, that my family can't take me, that my accomplishments can't take me, because when you've got the Christ ID card demons must let you through, people have to let you through. If the person you need to meet or the place you need to be is beyond a certain barrier that you're not qualified for, but Jesus wants you there; you will be there.

That's why I get consumed with who I am in Christ because I am where I am and I am who I am because of the grace of God. When I identify with him, my ID or my identification will get me places that nothing else can get me. Pride is an illusion that makes people believe that they can sustain their own lives. Do we not understand that we are incapable of doing anything outside the grace of God? It's crazy how people sin wilfully under God's grace and mercy. That's why pride is an illusion, it's an illusion that makes people think that they are capable of sustaining their own lives but not knowing that yes you may have a lot of money, yes you may have a lot of prestige, yes you may have a great family, and, yes you may have all these different things that make you beautiful and dope. But those things cannot sustain your eternal life. What's more important, your earthly life or your eternal life? Your earthly rewards or your eternal reward? But when you get so caught up on pride, you will neglect the things of God because you think that you're self-sufficient.

The number one thing that keeps people out of heaven is pride. Being gay does not make you go to hell, being a fornicator doesn't damn you to hell, adultery doesn't damn you to hell; pride does, that I'm not going to leave this lifestyle, I'm not going to let go of this way of thinking, I am not going to follow you because of my belief in the illusion that I can self-sustain myself. That's why it's important to be selfless. Selfishness kills. Selfishness kills relationships, selfishness kills communities, selfishness destroys churches, selfishness destroys families, selfishness is a cancer - all about me. Feed me, feed me, feed me, feed me versus I'm going to feed others because I know my Father will feed me. Imagine feeding or serving with no expectation of a return from that person. Imagine saying my God is so sufficient in me that I'm going to serve, through wisdom, people, my wife, my husband, my children and Im not going to expect them to give me anything in return, because the Holy Spirit will repay me either through them or supernaturally from somewhere else. We must trust that God will replenish us but when a person is selfish, they take, take, take but do not give. The best life to live is a giving life, giving through wisdom, giving based upon being led by God and giving with no expectation of return, unless you are in a contract of course.

The sole causes for pride are vanity, insecurities, an elevated self-confidence, vengeance and personal accomplishments. Let's start with vanity.

Vanity is the pursuit of things that have no point and have no value for eternity. Many people are pursuing vain things versus valid things. When a person is humble, they have a higher chance of seeing the true value behind things. Many people pursue things with no point because they have been blinded into thinking that things and people will fulfil their needs. Nevertheless, I love the scripture that says he will supply all of our needs according to his riches in glory. People want to be supplied based upon God's riches but not God's glory. God will not meet our "needs" through his riches if we do not have a heart that desires to give him the glory. A self-less person is going to make sure God is always magnified.
A selfish person is going to only come to God for selfish reasons and beg for God to supply their needs. God isn't going to supply your needs if he knows you're going to use that need for carnal reasons. God wants us to have a heart that wants validity not vanity. Many people are soul-tied to pursuits due to vanity. They are hoping that that pinnacle place of promotion will save them from where they are and who they are. No person, no product or no pinnacle can save you from you. Only Jesus can and once we see him for who he is and adopt his mindset we will be able to see the difference between what's vain and valid. Don't let vanity lure you into pursuing things that have no eternal value.

Number two, at the core of pride are insecurities. Because I am insecure, I have to feel or find things that will give me false security. False security is the façade of true security, a filling or form of security; but it's a partial security. Many people anchor their lives in things because they're insecure. I talk about my grades because I'm truly insecure, I talk about my accomplishments because deep down I'm secure, and I have to talk about these things to make me feel valid. It's crazy we'll puff up everything else to make us feel valid, but what truly makes us feel valid… Your grades did not create you, your accomplishments didn't create you, your boo didn't create you, your family didn't create you, your heritage didn't create you; God created you. That's where you find your dignity and your worth. When you know the creator, the created thing then begins to know their significance, their worth, and they will have dignity because of that.

An ambassador has dignity because they're speaking on behalf of a strong kingdom. Therefore, by us being ambassadors for the kingdom of God we can stand in any demonic realm and speak confidently because we're backed by the king of all kings and the kingdom of all kingdoms. Therefore, we receive our validity because of what Jesus did, because of his righteousness, because of what he did on the cross for us that's what makes us valid; the pursuit of everything else for validation is vain. So if you're not secured in the Gospel everything else will cause you to end up where there is no success, no true help or safety.

Elevated self-confidence. People elevate their self-confidence because of insecurity; they go together. These individuals elevate themselves to try and rise above issues they have yet to deal with. God designed for us to have a healthy confidence a confidence that is solely anchored in who they are in Christ. Many people are standing on the shoulders of their accomplishments, degrees, accolade who they know, etc instead of who they are in Christ. Those who stand on the shoulders of Jesus are extended above those on other shoulders.

People become prideful because of vengeance; they want to show their mom they did it, they want to show their dad they did it. If you live for the haters, you will die from their responses. You cannot live to prove to your haters that you succeeded; you succeed so that God gets the glory. What is the motive of your pursuit for success? What is your motive? Why are you chasing success? If you're going after it for vengeance to let that bully in high school know, to let your parents know, to let the world know, to let those people who thumbs down on your videos know, if you live by them you will miss out on celebrating with those who truly celebrate you. Do not go where you're tolerated; go where you're celebrated. You thrive where you're celebrated, you die where you're tolerated. So do not get so consumed with, "I got to prove. I want to prove, prove, prove." That's pride, that, "Look at me now, I'm somebody now, look what I've accomplished." trying to pull down the people who aren't even responsible for putting you up is vain. Why push down people who aren't even responsible for putting you up?

Personal accomplishments - people just want their lives full of accomplishments, they want people to hear about their seven Grammy's, their two Emmy's, their four championships, their five rings, their three degrees'. Your accomplishments do not make you, and if you keep going and going after accomplishment those things will only break you.

Now how do these things build soul-ties and, a stronghold?

I want to make sure I make this clear, there is nothing wrong with being proud of your accomplishments, family, degree etc. but when those things determine your identity that's when you fall. It's our responsibility to make sure we don't even allow the thought to creep in. What the enemy knows is that the best way to get pride in a person's heart is for there to be a hurt, a disappointment, a scar. When a person experiences a negative situation, that human being outside of the Gospel tends to try to prove to the naysayers that they're somebody. So in order to prove that they are somebody and that they have dignity and worth, they puff up these things to try to prove to everyone that they are somebody. But when a person has been liberated by Christ, those thoughts are now guarded through the filter that's in their mind letting them know that their significance and their worth is because of what Christ did for them. They no longer have to go down the path of trying to prove to others and to try to prove to themselves that they are somebody, but they know that they are somebody anyway solely because of Christ.

These things become strongholds because many people are too insecure because of what somebody has said about them, what has happened to them, what has happened to their people group, what has happened to their culture. Therefore, what happens, they feel like they have to be these saviours and they become so proud of it that they will defend those things before they defend the things of God. They become emotionally attached to it, because if you touch their accomplishments you touch their soul, if you touch their heritage you touch their soul, if you touch what they have that they love most that makes them who they are, that idolatry that's birthed out of pride if you touch it, they will kill, hurt and destroy you.

These strongholds become oak trees in people's lives and it's hard for them to let go because they're like, "But if I let go will people praise me? Will people say that I'm significant?" Listen man, which audience do you care about? The audience in this world or the heavenly hosts of angels who are celebrating and cheering you on? If you try to please people who aren't redeemed or trying to be redeemed, if you try to please them you'll die from their criticisms. However, if you are focused on making heaven rejoice and heaven proud you will obtain true success.

Let's look at some scriptures. Proverbs 11:2 and Proverbs 16:8 talks about the results of pride. **Proverbs 11:2** says *when pride comes then comes disgrace. But with the humble is wisdom.* **Proverbs 16:18** says, *Pride goes before destruction,* *and a haughty spirit before a fall.* The end of pride is destruction and the beginning of success is humility. You determine the end of a season by the pride or the humility you have in your heart. When pride comes, then comes disgrace. When a person walks in pride the proudness of their accomplishments etc. versus being humbled by what Christ did, then there will be disgrace. The moment a man or woman stands on their own merit they fall by their own merit. They're many people who started preaching the Gospel, started serving God and then the success came. The devil loves to feed success based on the world's terms. So what he does, he doesn't mind you being successful at YouTube subscriptions and followers, and being world renowned in your athletic endeavours, he don't care about you being successful. He cares about you using that success to succeed on behalf of God's kingdom. But if you're so consumed with your personal accomplishments and successes and not in advancing the kingdom of God, you're no threat to the enemy.

That's when people fall into disgrace because they're succeeding externally but they're not successful internally. God cares about your maturity, he cares about if you're able to manage what you're asking for. And if you can't manage it, God isn't going to bring it. But you can be lured to get it on your own because you have a free will. When you stand on your own merit destruction is imminent.

Proverbs 16:5 - *Everyone who is arrogant in heart is an abomination to the Lord. Be assured he will not go unpunished.* Have you ever heard people say, "I'm a God" or talk blasphemous against God's name? Those people will not go unpunished. That doesn't always mean that God punishes them, but their arrogance will punish them, their haughtiness will punish them, their atheistic beliefs will punish them, their blasphemous nature, and claiming to be a God will destroy them. That's why I tell people who think they're God, "Go create a world. Until you create a world, then come talk to me about you're a god." I am not talking about creating a world within a world; I'm not talking about creating a business, creating ideas, creating a culture. No, I am not talking about that. I am talking about creating a planet. Those people who think that way they will not go unpunished - either God'll punish them or their own arrogance will punish them.

Proverbs 29:23 - *One's pride will bring him low, but he who is lowly in spirit will obtain honour.* It's always best to start low than to end low; never forget that. I'd rather bring myself low being self-aware, than allowing my pride to bring me low. But if I'm lowly in spirit, humble in spirit, gentle in spirit, self-less in spirit then I will always obtain honour. My objective is to be the least in every room. Even if

I'm the best in the room, my job is to be the least - what I mean by that is not having low-self-esteem, but making sure I out serve everyone in the room. I'm going to make sure everyone feels happy that my presence is there. I'm not going to try to walk into the room as if I'm floating to the stage. I want to make sure that people know that I genuinely care I want to be the lowest person, the least person in the room. I'd rather push people up than to put people down, because the more you put people up they will turn around and help you go wherever you need to go.

Galatians 6:3 - *For if anyone thinks he is something when he is nothing he deceives himself.* **Proverbs 26:12** goes with it as well - *Do you see a man who is wise in his own eyes? There is more hope for a fool than him.* Pride is deceptive. When you think you are something when you are actually nothing in the grand scheme of things, you deceive yourself. It's crazy from God's vantage point a man that's homeless and a man in a Bentley still look like ants; small. It doesn't matter if you're in the first class of a plane or the back of the plane, if that plane crashes everybody in first class and coach dies the same death. So, when you know that you're nothing in the grand scheme of things and you're only somebody because of God, you will have a clear understanding and you won't be deceived.

Proverbs 27:2 - *Let another praise you and not your own mouth, a stranger and not your lips.* There's a difference between self-promotion versus stranger promotion. There is a principle - you will always go further when you let other people praise you; it is called word of mouth. If your arrogance precedes you then people's perception of you will precede them. But when you're truly humbled and you're letting God build you then you will let God boast for you. Let God build you up and let God boast for you; but you do neither. You continue to focus on submitting, working hard and being diligent and let God do the rest.

Self-promotion - you can only go as far as your ability to promote yourself, but when a stranger promotes you and they know you, and your work ethic, your mindset, your product and your creativity; their promotion will take you further. Work quietly and let someone else recognize your accomplishment. You work in silence and let them praise you publicly.

I love the scripture in **Jeremiah 9: 20-24**, which says - *Thus says the Lord let not the wise man boast in his wisdom, let not the mighty boast in their might, let not the rich boast in his riches. But let him who boast, boast in this, that he understands and knows me, that I am the Lord who practices steadfast love, justice and, righteousness on earth, for in these things I delight declares the Lord.*

There are three things that people typically find their pride in. They find pride in their wisdom, in their might, and in their riches. When a person boasts in their wisdom, their might, and their riches, they're boasting in the wrong thing. Our wisdom is nothing compared to God's wisdom. Our might is nothing in comparison to God's might, and our riches cannot buy us out of an eternal debt. Therefore, it is crazy how we boast in things that have limits. When I boast in my own wisdom I'll be haughty in my own intellectual understanding, and I'm always going to find myself deceived and looking stupid in comparison to God's wisdom. An earthly wisdom says it is best to "test-drive" a person sexually, move in with them so you can save money that sounds like wisdom; but that's man's wisdom. It makes sense to a lot of people; but it's not God's wisdom. God's wisdom is within the framework of the universe that when a person adheres to God's wisdom they get a better result than they would from man's wisdom, because man's wisdom is connected to the fallen part of the world. So why would I trust in man's wisdom that is flawed and fallen when I can trust in God's wisdom that is sure and sound.

You are only as strong as your spiritual might. You may be able to lift 400 lbs; you may have a lot of strength whether a woman or a man but your physical strength cannot out-lift the weight of spiritual warfare. The Bible says it's not by might but by my spirit says the Lord. You do not overcome by might. You overcome by the spirit's might. If the spirit of God is not using you, you will always fall when tested. And when you know God you know that money is fleeting, that you can have a bunch of money today, and no money tomorrow. When you are connected to God you have access to his riches, but we must always remember that his riches are for his purposes. When a person is doing work on behalf of someone else they are supplied with a certain amount of riches or money to do the work. God is not sitting there trying to give you a bunch of money that you will leave him, he gives you money for an assignment. But when you know you're connected to a God who owns cattle on a thousand hills you know you will be provide for. Back in the Bible days' cattle was currency and the hills were his provision for the cattle's strength, and when cattle are strengthened from all these pastures then that means that there is a lot of money, which implies that God can provide resources to sustain your multiple streams of income.

But the person who doesn't boast in these three things knows the Lord. That he is the Lord, who practices steadfast love, justice and righteousness on earth. These three things are essential for keeping us in peace. He is a steadfast and loving God, but also a God of justice. That you don't have to go out there and try to get vengeance, you don't have to try and go out there and get love; you don't have to work for your righteousness; it's all in him, and this is what the Lord delights in. Are you boasting in your wisdom, in your might, and in your riches? Or are you boasting in knowing God?

Let's look over some scriptures on vanity as well. **Proverbs 31:30** says, *Charm is deceitful, and beauty is vain but a woman who fears the Lord is to be praised.*

Many women in our culture are pursuing vanity, beauty, and charm; they're looking for these things to validate who they are. Because women have to deal with photo-shopped images, they have to face the world's opinion on beauty; and they feel like they have to chase this form of beauty to feel beautiful. That's why a woman's position as daughter will determine who she'll be as a woman in the marketplace, it will determine what kind of wife she'll be, what kind of mother she'll be, what kind of grandmother etc. When a woman doesn't know that she's a daughter of God, it doesn't matter how her father treated her, whether her dad was there or not, whether or not her dad was a good dad or a bad dad, if she doesn't know that she's God's daughter then she will be weak as a woman, weak as a wife, weak as a mother. Because she will be pursuing things that have no point, she'll be pursing vain things not valid things. The Bible says charm is deceitful beauty is vain, but a woman who fears the Lord is to be praised. This was a mother writing to her son letting him know that a woman can be full of charm, but that charm will be used to deceive you, that her beauty may be great, but that beauty will break down over time, that true beauty is in her heart. And that beauty becomes magnified when she fears the Lord. The fear of the Lord will lead her into the rivers of wisdom which will lead her into a mature woman, wife, business owner, ministry leader/supporter, community advocate etc. It all begins with her position as God's daughter. The pursuit of beauty is an internal search not an outward one. When a woman pursues the standards of beauty the way the world defines she will miss out on who she was created to be. There is nothing wrong with looking your best but if your outward appearance is your best side, then you are missing out on what true beauty is. Anything can happen to your face and many women breakdown the moment a blemish surfaces and this all boils down to the standards of the world. There is not a makeup line on the planet that can cover your inner girl.

This is for the men as well; it doesn't matter how handsome you are, how successful you are, you've got to fear the Lord because one car accident can take your handsomeness, one loss of a job can take your money; then who are you then?

Psalms 119:37 - *Turn my eyes from looking at worthless things and give me life in your way.* This is powerful. I love Psalms 119 because it's David really crying out for God's help, "God I need your help to turn my eyes." You've got to go before God, when you see a worthless thing and say, "God, I don't know if this is worth something or, worthless. However, God, if it is worthless, I need your help to turn my eye from it." This shows that you are completely dependent on the mercy, grace and, love of God to enable you to do what you can't do in your own strength." In your own strength, you can't turn your eye from worthless things. You need the supernatural strength of God to be able to turn your eye from worthless things. Do you have your eyes on worthless things? Do you have your eyes on things that's not going to benefit you in the grand scheme of things? If you are then you are not asking God enough or submitting to God enough for him to take your eyes off those things. The longer your eye is on that thing, the more you will listen to the suggestions of the enemy through that thing and overtime that thing will become a soul-tie.

There is not one person on this planet who has regrets doing things the Lord's way. They may have frustrations while doing it the Lord's way, but after they have done it His way they won't have regrets. A person who waited for the one that God had for them and had sex only in marriage has no regrets right now. They have no regrets because they did it his way, they have received life in doing it his way. And if you repent today, you can receive that same life even if you've made mistakes in your past. No one is perfect but you can be perfected by the one who is perfect!

1 Samuel 16:7 - *But the Lord said to Samuel, do not look on his appearance or on his height or his stature because I have rejected him. For the Lord see not as man sees, man looks on the outward appearance, but the Lord looks on the heart.* During Samuels, day and throughout history people wanted a king that had a great appearance, height and stature. However, God cares less about these things and weighs the heart. So many people are consumed with their appearance, their height and their stature, and with their beauty, their waist, and their figure. When a person is more consumed in these things they become rejected in God's eyes because they're telling God, "I am who I am because of the body I have, the stature I have, the height I have and the beauty and the appearance I have." The Bible continues to read that he told Samuel, he says, *For the Lord sees not as man sees* - God doesn't see things the way we see. We see things through carnal eyes; he sees things through holy eyes. And Samuel had to be instructed because he by habit, by tradition, would have selected a king off of those criteria's but when God corrected him he began to see as God saw, and was warned not to look on the outward appearance but to look and to discern the heart.

Listen, appearance, height, stature is rejected by God when they become your everything. Even if you are an attractive person with a good height and with a strong stature stay humble, because every stature, every appearance, every height under God's saving work is beautiful. But when you pursue these things you'll be vain. In addition, most people have chosen kings in their households more so by their appearance, their height and, stature instead of first a God fearing heart. And, now you're submitted to a man who only has a good appearance, height and who only has a good stature, but doesn't have the Holy Ghost, doesn't have any of the fruits of the spirit, and doesn't follow God with all of his heart. But you've got the girl who's attractive; you got the girl who has a nice height to your standard, you have a girl who has a nice body. But she doesn't have a strong mind; she has a weak heart, and she's insecure. You get what you choose that's why God says there's nothing wrong with liking appearance, height or stature, but they must come second to their heart. Before you invest in a person's appearance, stature or height, inspect their heart, because when you do that you will truly get that person who God has for you.

I'd rather have a person with a good heart than great appearance any day. But the good thing about God, God will also give you a person with a good submitted heart as well as the appearance you like, the stature and the height you like. Let God choose your king and let God choose your queen, but do not be consumed with outward appearance that you overlook the heart. Our world has conditioned us to only look externally than internally, that by the time you even look at that man or woman's heart you have already been infatuated, drawn into a sexual experience, been in engaged and married. And after all of this has happened and you have truly seen their character, it will be too late because you are either too tied to them to let them go or too deep in the situation to let them go. You must ask yourself - what kind of heart do I have and am I overly consumed with my appearance, my height, and my stature.

Pride					
How strong is the tie or hold in this area? →			Weak	Mild	Strong
Which areas are affected and in what way? Place a check beside each area that's affected and explain in what way in the larger box below.					
Spiritually	Mentally	Emotionally	Physically		

If you are struggling with your pride say the prayer below

Heavenly Father, I thank you for being my God, my provider my strength. I am glad that my identification is in you and that on my ID card is a slain lamb. I thank you for enabling me to humble myself under your mighty hand, trusting in your due season of promotion. God keep my heart from being arrogant, from being proud, and from identifying itself solely on things created than in the creator who is you. I repent for all my pride, and I break that pride in the spirit realm. God just like you said in your word for me to turn my eye from worthless things, God I'm asking you to turn my heart from worthless things. Lord, I pray right now that you will strengthen my heart, that you will cause my heart to love you. And I break this prideful connection demonically in the spirit realm. I will no longer pursue vain things or boast in my wisdom, riches and might for my joy is in the fact that I know you.

Right now through the authority that has been given to me through Christ Jesus I rebuke every spirit of pride and every spirit associated with it. I cancel every soul-tie and stronghold in my heart to pride, and I walk in my freedom today. I cancel my allegiance to my heritage; I cancel my allegiance to my skin colour, I cancel my allegiance to anything that supersedes my allegiance to God. In the name of Jesus, I am now free. Father God I thank you that your love will keep me as I endure in Jesus name. I love you Father, Amen!

THE FINALE – LET FREEDOM REIGN!

I pray this book was a blessing to you and I pray that you have reached freedom in levels untouchable by the enemy. I really hope and believe you're now like that bird flying out of that opened cage door flying into your freedom in Christ. That cage for those who have confessed Christ as Lord with fruit and true conversion evident, that door has been opened since the beginning. Ever since the veil was torn after his death between the outer courts to the holy of holies, that caged doors has been opened. Now we have access to the father, now we have access to freedom in Christ, and we now have access to flourish in our purpose! I really hope and believe that you have fought to gain this freedom and that you're fighting to maintain it.

Continue to pursue God and never forget that you are a pilgrim passing through, that you are a soldier in his army, and you must be watchful, prayerful and fasted in order to survive. If any of these things are neglected, you will fail. Maintaining this freedom is not going to be easy. Your enemy, those demons assigned to you are going to do whatever it takes to get you bound again; do not let them. Pursue freedom, embrace freedom, and thank Freedom every day that He reigns. Let freedom reign in your life; not ring, but **reign** and when you let that person reign in your life, then you will surely be freed indeed. – Whom the Son sets free is free indeed!

↑

GAMES AVAILABLE NOW AT MYCOACHJOSH.COM